Surf-side
EATING

Surf-side EATING

SIMPLE & FRESH RECIPES FOR SUMMER INSPIRED BY COASTAL LIVING

rps

RYLAND PETERS & SMALL
LONDON • NEW YORK

Senior Designer Toni Kay
Senior Editor Miriam Catley
Production Manager
  Gordana Simakovic
Art Director Leslie Harrington
Editorial Director Julia Charles
Publisher Cindy Richards
Indexer Vanessa Bird

First published in 2020.
This edition published in 2024 by
Ryland Peters & Small
20–21 Jockey's Fields, London
WC1R 4BW
and
341 E 116th St, New York NY 10029
www.rylandpeters.com

10 9 8 7 6 5 4 3 2 1

Text copyright © Valerie Aikman-
Smith, Vatcharin Bhumichitr, Jordan
Bourke, Tori Haschka, Atsuko Ikeda,
Kathy Kordalis, Louise Pickford,
James Porter, Shelagh Ryan, Laura
Santini and Janet Sawyer 2020, 2024
Design and photographs copyright
© Ryland Peters & Small 2020, 2024

ISBN: 978-1-78879-603-3

Printed in China

A CIP record for this book is available
from the British Library.

US Library of Congress
Cataloging-in-Publication Data
has been applied for.

NOTES:

• Both British (Metric) and American (Imperial plus US cups) measurements are included in these recipes for your convenience, however it is important to work with one set of measurements and not alternate between the two within a recipe.

• All spoon measurements are level unless otherwise specified.

• All eggs are medium (UK) or large (US), unless specified as large, in which case US extra-large should be used. Uncooked or partially cooked eggs should not be served to the very old, frail, young children, pregnant women or those with compromised immune systems.

• Ovens should be preheated to the specified temperatures. We recommend using an oven thermometer. If using a fan-assisted oven, adjust temperatures according to the manufacturer's instructions.

• When a recipe calls for the grated zest of citrus fruit, buy unwaxed fruit and wash well before using. If you can only find treated fruit, scrub well in warm soapy water before using.

OVEN METHOD FOR SEALING FILLED JARS

Preheat the oven to 250°F (120°C) Gas $\frac{1}{2}$. Pack the fruit or vegetables into sterilized jars leaving space at the top according to the recipe. Screw the lids on. Wipe the jars clean and, using jar tongs, place them in an oven-proof baking dish. Seal in the preheated oven for the specified time. Remove the dish from the oven and, using jar tongs, transfer the jars to a cooling rack. Leave undisturbed until they have cooled completely.

MIX
Paper from
responsible sources
FSC® C106563

Contents

Introduction

Whether you're chasing a wave, reaching for an endless summer or simply answering the call of the ocean, this book of bright and fresh recipes perfectly captures the spirit of the surf.

From the reward of a nourishing post-surf brunch to the simple pleasure of sipping a sundowner by the shore, this collection of relaxed recipes will evoke memories of the salty air and the soothing effect of time spent by the ocean. There's food here to enjoy from sunrise to sunset. In the first chapter, Rise & Shine, you'll discover perfect recipes to start each day – from smoothie bowls and toasted granola to sweet-savoury Maple & Bacon Pancakes and Corn Fritters with Smashed Avocado. For something vibrant yet light at lunch, head to Veggies, Salads & Sides and take a beach-side break with bowls of Miso-glazed Aubergine or Sweet Potato, Smoked Mackerel & Grapefruit. When the day calls for re-fueling with some tasty plates in between the surf, All-Day Dining includes Fish Tacos with Chipotle-lime Crema, Grilled Halloumi with a zingy Jalapeño, Lime & Tequila Relish and an Asian-inspired Yuzu Lomi Lomi Salmon Poke. Gather round the grill to cook delicious food to share from Beachside BBQ, such as Prawn & Beef Satays and Grilled Lobster – fresh from the day's catch – or create Sunset Suppers with of sweet-and-sour Summer Chicken or Thai-Steamed Snapper. Then, as you drift into the dusk, savour desserts that celebrate crisp, ripe produce such as Lychee Sorbet or Yogurt Panna Cotta, alongside a vodka Elderberry Snow Cone. Fresh, luscious and creative, these flavourful recipes are inspired by cuisines from the best beaches and surf spots around the globe including Australia, California, Hawaii, Thailand, Indonesia and beyond. So grab your board, or lazy lounger, and graze these delicious dishes from sunrise to sundown.

RISE & SHINE

WHIPPED HONEY VANILLA BUTTER

150 g/1¼ sticks salted butter, softened
1 teaspoon vanilla paste
2 tablespoons runny honey
bee pollen, to sprinkle

Place the softened butter, vanilla paste and honey in a bowl. Using a hand-held mixer, whisk the ingredients together until light and fluffy. Serve sprinkled with bee pollen.

Grainy porridge

This is an earthier version of traditional porridge, made using ancient grains.

50 g/¼ cup quinoa
100 g/½ cup amaranth
100 g/½ cup millet
a pinch of salt
450 ml/scant 2 cups almond, coconut or oat milk of your choice, plus extra to serve

pumpkin seeds
goji berries
nuts
honey
Whipped Honey Vanilla Butter (see right)
Glow Balls (see right)

TO SERVE
almond, coconut or oat milk
bee pollen

MAKES 6
SMALL BOWLS
or 3 large bowls

Bring the quinoa, amaranth, millet, salt, non-dairy milk and 450 ml/scant 2 cups water to the boil in a medium pan. Reduce the heat, partially cover and simmer, stirring occasionally, until the cereal is the consistency of porridge (softer and thicker than the usual bowl of oatmeal) and water is absorbed, approx. 40–50 minutes. If you want a looser, creamier texture, add more milk at this stage. Serve with your choice of the toppings, RIGHT.

GLOW BALLS

Brazil nuts are an excellent source of complex B vitamins. With the addition of the power spice turmeric, cocoa nibs and bee pollen, these balls will have you glowing inside and out. Make a batch and freeze them. They are a perfect snack or a fun porridge topper.

200 g/1½ cups Brazil nuts
100 g/¾ cup dates, pitted
100 g/¾ cup dried figs
1 tablespoon desiccated/dried unsweetened shredded coconut
2 tablespoons coconut oil
½ teaspoon ground turmeric

½ teaspoon ground cinnamon
4 cardamom pods, ground
2 tablespoons ground flax seeds
1 tablespoon cocoa nibs
½ tablespoon bee pollen

MAKES 40
(teaspoon size)

In a food processor place the Brazil nuts, dates, figs, desiccated/dried unsweetened shredded coconut, coconut oil, turmeric, cinnamon, cardamom and flax seeds and blitz into a textured paste. Transfer into a bowl and mix in the cocoa nibs and bee pollen. Form into 40 balls. Store in the fridge until needed.

Toasted muesli WITH BAKED RHUBARB

Fill your shopping bag with oats, barley, nuts, seeds, and dried fruit, mix all the ingredients together and slowly toast them in the oven. Store it in a glass jar on the kitchen counter to admire: a breakfast of champions.

100 ml/⅓ cup sunflower oil
½ teaspoon pure vanilla extract
125 ml/⅓ cup clear honey
125 ml/½ cup maple syrup
¼ teaspoon ground cinnamon
500 g/2½ cups jumbo rolled oats
150 g/1½ cups rolled barley flakes
70 g/⅔ cup wheatgerm
50 g/⅔ cup shredded/desiccated coconut
125 g/1¼ cup almonds
100 g/1 cup pecans
125 g/scant 1 cup sunflower seeds
100 g/⅔ cup pumpkin seeds
10 g/1 tablespoon sesame seeds
250 g/1⅔ cup (dark) raisins
200 g/1½ cup dried dates, halved
Greek yogurt, to serve

BAKED RHUBARB
500 g/5 cups rhubarb, trimmed and
    cut into 5-cm/2-inch pieces
2 tablespoons caster/granulated sugar
freshly squeezed juice and grated zest
    of 1 orange
2 baking sheets, greased and lined
    with baking parchment
sterilized glass jars with airtight lids
    (optional)

SERVES 10

Preheat the oven to 130°C (250°F) Gas ½.

Pour the oil, vanilla, honey, syrup and cinnamon into a saucepan or pot set over a gentle heat and stir to combine.

Mix together all the remaining ingredients, except the (dark) raisins, dates and yogurt in a large mixing bowl. Pour over the hot oil mixture and stir well to ensure everything is well coated.

Spread the mixture evenly onto the prepared baking sheets and bake in the preheated oven for 30–45 minutes. Stir the mixture at regular intervals and cook until evenly golden and dry. Remove from the oven and set aside to cool completely before adding the reserved (dark) raisins and dates.

To make the Baked Rhubarb, preheat the oven to 150°C (300°F) Gas 2. Place the rhubarb in a baking pan that is big enough to hold it in a single layer. Sprinkle over the sugar, orange juice and zest, and gently mix together. Cover with foil and bake in the preheated oven for 30–45 minutes, until the rhubarb is just soft. Remove from the oven and set aside to cool completely before serving with the toasted muesli and Greek yogurt.

Store any leftover muesli and baked rhubarb in separate airtight containers or sterilized glass jars fitted with airtight lids. The muesli will keep at room temperature for up to 2 weeks and the rhubarb should be kept in the fridge for 3–5 days.

Savoury granola

Delicious for breakfast with thick Greek yogurt, mango, avocado and even a handful of chopped coriander/cilantro and a little bit of olive oil.

90 g/1 cup rolled oats
60 g/½ cup pistachios, shelled
60 g/½ cup walnuts, roughly quartered
60 g/7 tablespoons sunflower seeds
40 g/5 tablespoons sesame seeds
½ tablespoon fennel seeds
½ tablespoon coriander seeds
20 g/³⁄₄ oz. cacao nibs
½ teaspoon cayenne pepper
1 teaspoon sea salt flakes
2 rosemary sprigs, leaves only, roughly chopped
1 tablespoon freshly grated lemon zest
4 tablespoons olive oil
1 tablespoons maple syrup
1 tablespoon soy sauce
1 large egg white, lightly beaten

SERVES 2–3

Preheat the oven to 180°C (360°F) Gas 4.

Combine the oats, nuts, seeds and cacao nibs in a large bowl. Sprinkle over the cayenne pepper, salt, rosemary and lemon zest and give it a good mix. Add the olive oil, maple syrup, soy sauce and mix thoroughly again.

Finally mix in the beaten egg white and combine. Spread the mixture in a thin layer on a non-stick baking sheet.

Bake for 20–25 minutes, stirring a couple of times, until just nicely golden brown. Keep a close eye on the mixture as the seeds can burn very quickly.

Allow the granola to cool and then serve with a good dollop of Greek yogurt. The granola will keep for two weeks in a sealed plastic container.

Blackberry & blueberry açai bowl

As a food, açai pulp from the tribal Amazon belt is often blended with the starchy root vegetable manioc and eaten as porridge. The taste is often described as reminiscent of wild berries and chocolate. The addition of it in powdered form in a smoothie and blended with fresh berries gives you a great start to the day.

200 ml/scant 1 cup coconut water
2 ripe bananas (if you have a Nutribullet, you could put them chopped into the freezer and add them straight from there for a creamier texture)
100 g/½ cup frozen blueberries
50 g/¼ cup frozen blackberries
1 tablespoon açai powder
1 tablespoon oats, gluten free if you wish, to make it a bit thicker and creamier (optional)

TO SERVE
100 g/³⁄₄ cup blueberries
50 g/⅓ cup blackberries
1 dragon fruit, cleaned and sliced
50 g/⅓ cup kiwiberries or 1 whole kiwi, cleaned and sliced
1 tablespoon slivered pistachios
a few sprigs of mint

SERVES 4 in small bowls

Blend the coconut water, bananas, frozen berries and açai powder together in a blender until smooth. Stand for a few minutes to thicken. Spoon into 4 small serving bowl. Arrange the fresh fruit, pistachios and mint on top and serve.

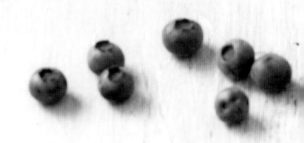

Maple & bacon pancakes

What's not to like about the combination of pancakes, bacon and maple syrup?

125 g/1 cup plain/all-purpose flour, (spooned and levelled)
2 teaspoons caster/granulated sugar
1½ teaspoons baking powder
½ teaspoon bicarbonate of/baking soda
½ teaspoon salt
310 ml/1¼ cups buttermilk

2 tablespoons unsalted butter, melted
1 UK large, US extra large egg
10 rashers/slices streaky/fatty bacon
pure maple syrup, to serve (optional)

MAKES 10

Preheat the oven to 200°C (400°F) Gas 6. In a bowl, whisk together the flour, sugar, baking powder, bicarbonate of/baking soda and salt. In another bowl, whisk together the buttermilk, butter and egg. Mix the flour mixture into the buttermilk mixture until just combined, with small to medium lumps remaining.

In a large non-stick frying pan/skillet, fry the bacon until golden on both sides and just turning crisp. Drain the bacon on paper towels and set aside.

Make each bacon pancake by dropping a tablespoon of batter into the pan/skillet, top with a bacon rasher/slice, and cover with a further teaspoon of batter. Cook until some bubbles appear on top of the pancake and a few have burst, 1½–2 minutes. With a spatula, carefully flip the pancake and cook until golden. Repeat with all the bacon rashers/slices, cooking in batches if necessary and keeping the cooked pancakes warm in a low oven. Make more pancakes in the same way with any remaining batter, adding more oil to the pan if necessary. Serve with maple syrup if desired.

Sweet potato pancakes
WITH CINNAMON & VANILLA

Sweet pancakes with a healthy twist, the perfect way to start the day.

300 g/10 oz. sweet potato, peeled and chopped
125 g/1 cup plain/all-purpose flour
1 teaspoon baking powder
1 teaspoon ground cinnamon
3–4 tablespoons caster/superfine sugar
1 tablespoon vanilla extract
125 ml/½ cup milk

1 egg, beaten
1 tablespoon butter, melted and slightly cooled
vegetable or groundnut oil, for frying
natural/plain yogurt, stewed apples and maple syrup, or vanilla ice cream, to serve

SERVES 4–6

Bring a pan of water to the boil and steam the sweet potatoes until tender, then drain and leave to cool. Meanwhile, sift the flour, baking powder and cinnamon into a large mixing bowl. Stir in the sugar. Add the vanilla extract to the milk and egg, along with the melted butter. Gradually add the wet ingredients to the dry, combining it all together with a fork. The batter can be made up to 24 hours in advance and stored in the fridge in a bowl, covered, if you like.

Before cooking, mash the sweet potatoes, then stir them through the batter until well combined. Melt a little oil in a non-stick frying pan/skillet over fairly high heat. Once hot, carefully add heaped tablespoons of the batter. Gently fry until golden brown on both sides, turning them with a spatula.

Serve stacked with yogurt, stewed apples and maple syrup.

Apple & blueberry waffles

Waffles are a great breakfast or brunch treat, and this recipe is a refreshing diversion from the usual flavour combinations associated with them. Do not add too much fat, sugar or egg to the waffle mixture, or they will go soft soon after cooking.

FOR THE WAFFLES
1 vanilla pod/bean
250 ml/1 cup milk
250 g/2 cups plain/all-purpose flour, sifted
2 teaspoons baking powder
½ teaspoon salt
½ teaspoon ground cardamom (optional)
2 tablespoons sugar
200 g/13 tablespoons butter
250 ml/1 cup whipping cream
6 eggs, beaten

FOR THE TOPPING
1 large apple
150 g/generous 1 cup blueberries
½ a cinnamon stick
1 star anise
2 whole cloves
300 ml/1⅓ cups pomegranate, grape or cranberry juice
vanilla yogurt and fresh fruit, to serve

waffle iron (optional)

SERVES 12

To make the waffles, split the vanilla pod/bean in half lengthways, then put it in a small pan with the milk, heat gently and set aside for at least 30 minutes. In a bowl, mix all the dry ingredients together. Melt the butter in a small pan. Add the butter and infused milk (discard the pod/bean), with the cream and eggs, to the dry ingredients and whisk lightly until a batter consistency is formed. Leave the batter to rest for around 30 minutes, or overnight in the refrigerator if possible.

Meanwhile, make the topping. Remove the cores from the apples and slice them, keeping the skins on. Place them, along with the other topping ingredients, in a pan and cook until the apple and blueberries are soft, about 3–4 minutes. Remove the fruit with a slotted spoon and set aside. Boil the remaining juices for 10–15 minutes, until a syrup consistency is reached. Strain the syrup to remove the spices, then return it to the pan to cook gently for a further 2 minutes, with the fruit. You can then blend the mixture if you like, or keep the fruit whole.

Heat a waffle iron over medium heat. Spoon the mixture into the iron, just up to the top. Cook the waffle until it is a golden colour, then remove and cool on a wire rack until ready to serve. To serve, pour the fruit over the waffles, adding a blob of something creamy, such as vanilla yogurt, and a handful of fresh red fruit.

French toast WITH HONEY ROAST FIGS, ORANGE MASCARPONE & TOASTED ALMONDS

Nothing says 'Saturday morning' better than French toast. The orange mascarpone cuts perfectly through the thick, eggy brioche and you can flavour the figs with your favourite honey – rose, vanilla and ginger all work well.

125 ml/½ cup mascarpone
2 tablespoons single/light cream
½ teaspoon grated orange zest,
    plus extra to serve
1 tablespoon freshly squeezed
    orange juice
4 ripe figs, cut in half lengthways
clear honey, to drizzle
100 g/3½ oz. whole almonds
2 eggs
100 ml/½ cup milk
¼ teaspoon pure vanilla extract
1 tablespoons caster/granulated sugar
2–4 thick slices of brioche
unsalted butter, for frying
icing/confectioners' sugar, for dusting
2 baking sheets, greased and
    lined with baking parchment

SERVES 2

Preheat the oven to 180°C (350°F) Gas 4.

Mix the mascarpone with the cream, orange zest and juice in a small mixing bowl. Cover and set aside or in the fridge until you are ready to serve.

Place the figs, cut-side up, on one of the prepared baking sheets. Drizzle with honey and roast in the preheated oven for 15–20 minutes until soft and caramelized. Remove from the oven and set aside until you are ready to serve.

Meanwhile, scatter the almonds on the other baking sheet and bake in the same oven for 8–10 minutes until lightly golden. Remove from the oven, cool completely then roughly chop.

To make the French toast, whisk together the eggs with the milk in a large mixing bowl. Add the vanilla and caster/granulated sugar, and whisk again. Transfer to a shallow dish and set aside.

Melt a little butter in a large frying pan/skillet set over a medium heat.

Dip each slice of brioche in the egg mixture one at a time. Let the slices soak up the egg mixture for a few seconds, then turn over to coat the other side.

Place the egg-soaked brioche slices in the hot pan and cook until golden on the bottom. Turn over and cook for a few minutes longer until each side is golden. Transfer to a clean baking sheet and put in the still-warm oven to keep warm while you cook the remaining slices. Cook the remaining toasts in the same way, adding a little more butter to the pan each time, if required.

To serve, cut the brioche in half diagonally. Overlap the triangles on the plate and top with the honey roast figs, orange mascarpone and toasted almonds. Sprinkle with a little extra orange zest and dust with icing/confectioners' sugar.

Banana bread WITH RASPBERRY LABNE

Banana bread is absolutely delicious on its own or toasted with butter but if you want an indulgent start to the day, try it with this beautiful Raspberry Labne. Labne is a strained yogurt which has a consistency somewhere between cream cheese and yogurt. The longer you leave it, the firmer it becomes so play around with the consistency.

125 g/1 stick unsalted butter, softened
250 g/1¼ cups caster/granulated sugar
2 large eggs, beaten
1 teaspoon pure vanilla extract
250g/2 cups plain/all-purpose flour
2 teaspoons baking powder
4 very ripe bananas, mashed

RASPBERRY LABNE
150 g/1 generous cup fresh
    or frozen raspberries
100 g/½ cup caster/granulated sugar
500 g/2 cups Greek yogurt
1 teaspoon pure vanilla extract
*a 900-g/2-lb loaf pan, greased and
    lined with baking parchment*
*2 fine mesh sieves/strainers,
    1 lined with several layers
    of muslin/cheesecloth*

**MAKES 8 SLICES
AND SERVES 4**

Preheat the oven to 180°C (350°F) Gas 4.

Beat the butter and caster/granulated sugar together in a large mixing bowl until light, fluffy and a pale cream colour. Gradually beat in the eggs, one at a time, before adding the vanilla.

In a separate bowl, sift together the flour and baking powder.

Gently fold the mashed bananas into the wet mixture a little at a time, alternating with the sifted flour mixture so that the mixture doesn't split.

Transfer the banana batter to the prepared loaf pan, then bake in the preheated oven for 20 minutes.

Reduce the oven temperature to 160°C (325°F) Gas 3 and cook for a further 40–45 minutes until golden brown, firm to the touch and a skewer inserted into the middle comes out clean.

Set aside to cool in the pan for 5 minutes then turn out onto a wire rack to cool completely.

To make the Raspberry Labne, place 50 g/½ cup of the raspberries in a small saucepan or pot with the sugar and 100 ml/scant ½ cup of water. Set over a gentle heat and simmer until it reduces by one-third.

Remove from the heat and strain through the unlined sieve/strainer set over a mixing bowl. Discard the raspberry pulp, cover the syrup and set aside to cool completely.

Add the yogurt, cooled raspberry syrup, vanilla and remaining raspberries, and mix together. Pour the mixture into the lined sieve/strainer set over a mixing bowl. Draw the cloth together, twist the gathered cloth to form a tight ball and tie the ends with kitchen string. Suspend the wrapped labne over the bowl and set in the fridge for 12–24 hours. Discard the drained water and transfer the labne to a bowl, ready to serve with slices of banana bread.

Corn fritters

WITH ROAST TOMATOES & SMASHED AVOCADOS

Corn fritters are a menu staple in nearly every café in Australia and New Zealand. No two recipes are ever the same as everyone has their (strong!) opinion on what makes the perfect fritter.

150 g/2 cups (about 1 medium) grated courgette/zucchini
sea salt and freshly ground black pepper, to season
400 g/2½ cups cherry vine tomatoes
olive oil, to drizzle
4 eggs
180 g/1⅓ cups self-raising/rising flour
50 g/1¾ oz. Parmesan, grated
100 ml/scant ½ cup buttermilk
1 teaspoon paprika
½ teaspoon cayenne pepper
1 tablespoon chopped coriander/cilantro
fresh corn kernels cut from 2–3 cobs
sunflower oil, for frying

SMASHED AVOCADOS
3 avocados
freshly squeezed juice of 2 limes and the grated zest of 1
¼ red onion, finely diced
1 teaspoon hot sauce

TO SERVE
fresh spinach
crème fraîche

SERVES 6

Put the grated courgette/zucchini into a colander set over a large mixing bowl. Sprinkle with ½ teaspoon of salt and leave for 30 minutes–1 hour so they release their moisture. Squeeze the grated courgette/zucchini with your hands to get rid of as much moisture as possible and set aside.

For the roast tomatoes, preheat the oven to 180°C (350°F) Gas 4. Place the tomatoes on a baking sheet, drizzle with olive oil and season with salt and pepper.

Roast in the preheated oven for 15–20 minutes, or until the skins begin to split.

Reduce the oven temperature to 170°C (325°F) Gas 3 and prepare the fritter batter. In a large, clean, dry mixing bowl, lightly whisk the eggs. Add in the flour, grated Parmesan, buttermilk, paprika, cayenne pepper, ½ teaspoon of salt, a pinch of pepper and chopped coriander/cilantro.

Stir in the squeezed courgette/zucchini and corn kernels, ensuring the vegetables are evenly coated in batter.

Add enough sunflower oil to thinly cover the bottom of a heavy-bottomed frying pan/skillet. Ladle generous spoonfuls of batter into the pan and cook for about 4 minutes on each side, until golden brown. Transfer to a clean baking sheet and put in the still-warm oven for 4–5 minutes to ensure they are cooked through. Cook the remaining batter in the same way, adding a little more oil to the pan each time, if required.

Just before serving, roughly mash the avocados with a fork, leaving them fairly chunky. Stir in the lime juice and zest, onion and hot sauce. Season generously with salt and serve with the fritters, roast tomatoes, a handful of fresh spinach and a dollop of crème fraîche.

Sourdough toast toppings

A brown rye sourdough works well with both sweet or savoury or somewhere in between. Buy a good sourdough from your local bakery and serve with any of the following toppings.

CRUSHED BERRIES & GOAT'S CURD

500 g/3 cups frozen berries
2 tablespoons sugar
1 teaspoon vanilla paste
100 g/³/4 cup goat's curd, to serve

Place the berries, sugar and vanilla paste in a saucepan and heat gently, crushing the berries with a fork. Do not overcook as you want to retain some texture. Serve with the goat's curd.

AVOCADO & SALMON

2–3 avocados, peeled, stoned/pitted and sliced
200 g/1 cup smoked salmon
a handful of large capers
lemon, sliced, to serve

Assemble the ingredients on a large platter and allow your guests to top their own toast with the avocados, salmon, capers and a slice of lemon.

BROAD BEAN, COURGETTE & GOAT'S CURD

1 tablespoon olive oil
1 courgette/zucchini, thinly
   sliced into half moons
2 spring onions/scallions, sliced
150 g/1¼ cups frozen broad/
   fava beans, defrosted and
   skins removed
a handful of parsley,
   finely chopped
a handful of chives,
   finely chopped
juice of ¹/2 lemon
grated zest of 1 lemon
100 g/³/4 cup goat's curd,
   to serve
sea salt and freshly ground
   black pepper

Heat the oil in a frying pan/skillet. Add the courgette/zucchini, spring onions/scallions and broad/fava beans. Cook for 10 minutes – they should be just cooked and retain some bite. Place in a bowl and finish with the herbs, lemon juice and zest, goat's curd and season with salt and pepper.

Courgette loaf

This is a great alternative to savoury muffins in the morning. Its loaf shape makes it easy to toast – thick slices, lightly toasted under a grill/broiler then spread with butter and jam beat savoury muffins hands down.

300 g/4 cups (about 2) grated courgette/zucchini
300 g/2²/₃ cups self-raising/ rising flour, sifted
1 teaspoon baking powder
1 teaspoon mustard powder
¹/₂ teaspoon sea salt
¹/₂ teaspoon cayenne pepper
170 g/1²/₃ cups grated strong/ sharp Cheddar
100 g/6¹/₂ tablespoons butter, melted
4 eggs, beaten
135 mL/¹/₂ cup plus 1 tablespoon milk
a 900-g/2-lb loaf pan, greased and lined with baking parchment

MAKES 8 SLICES AND SERVES 4

Preheat the oven to 180°C (350°F) Gas 4.

Squeeze the grated courgette/zucchini with your hands to get rid of as much moisture as possible and place in a large mixing bowl with the flour, baking powder, mustard powder, salt, cayenne pepper and grated Cheddar. Toss everything together gently with your hands.

Combine the melted butter with the beaten eggs and milk in a jug/pitcher. Pour over the courgette/zucchini mixture and gently combine using a large spoon. Take care not to overwork the mixture – you should have a thick batter.

Spoon the mixture into the prepared loaf pan and bake in the preheated oven for 50 minutes–1 hour, until golden brown and a skewer inserted into the middle comes out clean.

Set aside to cool in the pan for 5 minutes then turn out onto a wire rack to cool completely.

Slice, toast and butter the cornbread to serve.

VEGGIES,
SALADS & SIDES

Miso-glazed aubergine

This traditional dish has found its way onto most modern izakaya and Japanese restaurant menus. The sweet and savoury umami flavours coupled with the melty texture of the grilled aubergine/eggplant make it sublimely satisfying. The best way to eat this is to scoop out the miso-caramelly flesh with a spoon.

2 aubergines/eggplants
4 tablespoons toasted sesame oil
4 tablespoons vegetable oil
1 tablespoon crushed roasted hazelnuts, to serve

DENGAKU MISO GLAZE
5 tablespoons brown rice miso
2 tablespoons soft light brown sugar
1 tablespoon mirin
1 tablespoon sake

MAKES 8

Peel strips of skin off the aubergines/eggplants lengthways, (alternately leaving a strip, then peeling a strip) to create a striped pattern. Top and tail each aubergine/eggplant, then slice each one widthways into 3-cm/1¼-inch thick round slices.

Use a sharp knife to score a cross-hatch pattern onto each side of the aubergine/eggplant slices. This technique is called a 'hidden cut', and it helps the vegetables to cook quickly and lets flavours penetrate.

Preheat the grill/broiler to 180°C (350°F) or to the medium-heat setting.

Place the aubergine/eggplant slices on a baking sheet and drizzle with the toasted sesame oil and vegetable oil.

Grill/broil the vegetables for 15 minutes until lightly browned and tender.

In the meantime, make the dengaku miso glaze. Combine the brown rice miso, brown sugar, mirin and sake with 1½ tablespoons of water in a small saucepan. Simmer over a low heat for 1 minute, stirring with a spatula, until the mixture is combined and glossy. Set aside.

When the aubergine/eggplant slices are lightly browned and tender, remove them from the grill/broiler and spread the miso glaze on top. Return to the grill/broiler for 4–5 minutes, or until bubbling.

Sprinkle the aubergine/eggplant slices with crushed roasted hazelnuts to serve.

Ouzo watermelon salad

Serve this refreshingly simple, eye-catching salad when the mercury starts to rise. The ouzo infuses the watermelon just a little, enhancing all that sweet goodness. It's the perfect salad to pack up and take to the beach to enjoy while watching the sun set.

1 watermelon
120 ml/½ cup ouzo
4 Persian cucumbers
450 g/1 lb. feta cheese, crumbled
130 g/1 cup pitted/stoned Kalamata
   olives
60 ml/¼ cup extra virgin olive oil
small bunch oregano
sea salt and cracked black pepper

SERVES 6

Place the watermelon on a work surface and cut into quarters. Remove the skin, cut the flesh into 4-cm/1½-inch cubes, and place in a large bowl.

Pour the ouzo over the watermelon and gently toss together to make sure all the pieces are coated. Marinate for 20 minutes.

Chop the cucumber into 4-cm/1½-inch chunks and add to the watermelon. Add the feta and olives and pour over the olive oil. Season with the salt and pepper and gently toss to combine.

Serve on a large platter and scatter with oregano leaves.

Quinoa & asparagus salad WITH MATCHA LEMON DRESSING

SALAD
100 g/½ cup black or red quinoa
sea salt
2 tablespoons olive oil
a bunch of asparagus spears,
  woody ends cut off
4 oranges
2 large avocados
1 large red onion, finely sliced
handful of mint, roughly
  chopped
handful of basil, roughly
  chopped
4 large handfuls rocket/arugula
  leaves

DRESSING
1 garlic clove, crushed
freshly squeezed juice of
  1 lemon
½ teaspoon matcha green tea
pinch of wasabi paste or
  powder, to taste (optional)
sea salt and freshly ground
  black pepper
7 tablespoons extra virgin
  olive oil

TO SERVE
1 handful toasted pumpkin
  seeds

SERVES 4

This vibrant and luscious salad is packed with antioxidants and healthful flavours. To taste the real benefits of this vital vinaigrette, try to use a good cold-pressed extra virgin olive oil.

Rinse the quinoa in cold water and then cook in a large saucepan of salted boiling water for about 12–20 minutes (depending on the colour) until the grains become soft but still have some bite.

Meanwhile, make the dressing by combining all the ingredients apart from the oil in a bowl and then whisk in the oil. Season to taste and set aside.

Once the quinoa is cooked, drain, stir through a little olive oil to stop it from sticking together and set aside to cool.

Steam or boil the asparagus until cooked and the stalks are al dente. Remove from the heat, drain and refresh under cold running water to fix the colour and set aside. Slice each stalk on the diagonal into thumb-length spears.

With a sharp knife cut down the sides of the oranges to remove the skin and pith and slice the orange into 1 cm/½ inch discs. Save any juice from the oranges to add to your dressing.

Peel and cut the avocados into large chunks.

Put all the salad ingredients, including the herbs and rocket/arugula, into a large serving dish and then toss together.

To serve, pour the dressing (adding any reserved orange juice first) onto the salad and combine well.

Serve with a scattering of toasted pumpkin seeds.

Vegetables WITH SPICY DIP OF YOUNG CHILLIES

4 large fresh green chillies/chiles

4 small fresh green chillies/chiles

6 large garlic cloves

6 pink Thai shallots or 3 regular ones

4 medium tomatoes

2 tablespoons freshly squeezed lime or lemon juice

2 tablespoons light soy sauce

½ teaspoon salt

2 teaspoons sugar

TO SERVE

your choice of crisp lettuce, cucumber, radishes, celery or other raw or blanched vegetables

SERVES 4

Thai dips are mostly made from chillies. You find them in all regions of Thailand – served with raw or boiled vegetables, sticky rice in the north and steamed rice in the region of Central Thailand. This dip, as its name implies, is made from young, green, strongly flavoured chillies and is wonderful used both as dipping sauces, and as sauces for spooning over rice or other dishes.

Wrap the chillies/chiles, garlic, shallots and tomatoes in foil and put under a preheated medium grill/broiler. Cook until they begin to soften, turning once or twice. Unwrap, then pound with a mortar and pestle to form a liquid paste.

Add the lemon juice, soy sauce, salt and sugar to the paste, stirring well, then spoon into a small dipping bowl.

Serve as a dipping sauce, surrounded by crisp salad ingredients, such as lettuce, cucumber, radish and celery, or with raw or blanched vegetables.

Note In Thailand, seeds from chillies/chiles are rarely discarded, but you can do so if you wish. All chillies/chiles vary in heat, so adjust according to your preference.

Shaved fennel salad

WITH WALNUTS, PARMESAN & POMEGRANATE

Using a mandolin to slice vegetables will transform your salads – courgettes/zucchini, fennel and carrots are all delicious raw and dressed simply with lemon juice and olive oil.

4 tablespoons olive oil, plus extra to serve

3 tablespoons freshly squeezed lemon juice

grated zest of 1 lemon

15 g/1/4 cup chopped chives

1/2 teaspoon sea salt

freshly ground black pepper, to season

600 g/1 1/4 lbs. (about 2 medium) fennel bulbs, trimmed and finely sliced

1 pear, cored, quartered and thinly sliced

seeds of 1 pomegranate

60 g/2/3 cup walnuts, toasted

60 g/1 cup Parmesan shavings

70 g/1 1/4 cup rocket/arugula

SERVES 6

Begin by whisking the oil together with the lemon juice and zest in a large mixing bowl. Add the chopped chives, salt and pepper to taste.

Add the sliced fennel and pear, and gently toss in the dressing to prevent any discolouration.

Add the remaining ingredients, one at a time, and gently mix together.

Serve with an extra drizzle of olive oil.

Grated carrots, blood orange & walnuts

The colour of this blood orange salad is enough to win anyone over, but it is full of flavour as well. It's perfect as a side or with a number of other salads, all sumptuously laid out together. Get your hands on blood oranges while they are in season.

2 blood oranges

8 large carrots, grated

grated zest and juice of 1 lemon

3 tablespoons agave syrup

1 tablespoon freshly chopped parsley

4 tablespoons extra virgin olive oil

sea salt

2 handfuls of walnuts, fresh from the shell

SERVES 6

Cut the top and bottom off the oranges, just down to the flesh, then place the orange on its end, cut side down, and carefully, following the shape of the orange, cut the peel off in strips from top to bottom, making sure you cut off the white pith too. Then turn them on their side and cut them into 1-cm/3/8-inch thick rounds. Do this on a board or somewhere that will catch any orange juice that you inadvertently squeeze out of them; this can be added to the dish too.

Squeeze any excess juice out of the grated carrots to prevent the salad from being too soggy (you can drink any juice you extract). In a large bowl, combine the carrots with all the other ingredients. This should be a punchy, citrussy salad with just enough sweetness from the agave. Let all the flavours combine together for 15 minutes, then taste again, adjust the seasoning with more juice, parsley, salt and agave if necessary.

Grilled squid salad WITH HERB LIME DRESSING

This is such a pretty salad with the different layers yielding many different flavours, colours and textures. It is also delicious with prawns/shrimp. Use peeled green ones with the tail on and grill them the same way as the squid.

2 red (bell) peppers
800 g/1¾ lbs. cleaned squid
2 heads of chicory, leaves removed
   and cut in half lengthways
30 g/½ cup baby spinach leaves
40 g/¼ cup edamame or broad/fava
   beans (fresh or frozen), blanched
10 g/scant ¼ cup coriander/cilantro

DRESSING
freshly squeezed juice of 2 limes
30 ml/2 tablespoons olive oil
20 g/2 tablespoons palm sugar
1 garlic clove, grated
30 g/½ cup finely chopped
   coriander/cilantro
15 g/¼ cup finely chopped basil
30 ml/2 tablespoons fish sauce
1 long fresh red chilli/chile, deseeded
   and finely chopped
freshly ground black pepper, to season
a baking sheet, lined with foil

SERVES 4

Preheat the oven to 200°C (400°F) Gas 6.

Begin by roasting the red (bell) peppers. Place on the prepared baking sheet and roast in the preheated oven for 20 minutes. Turn and roast for a further 20 minutes until the peppers collapse and the skin is charred and soft. Transfer to a small mixing bowl, cover with clingfilm/plastic wrap and set aside. When the peppers are cool enough to handle, remove and discard the skin and seeds, and slice.

To make the herb lime dressing, combine all the ingredients in a small mixing bowl using a whisk. It is important to make the dressing by hand rather than using a blender as you want the dressing to have texture.

To prepare the squid, cut off but reserve the tentacles and cut down the 'seam' of the squid so it opens out flat. Score the inside with a cross-hatch pattern, then slice lengthways into 2-cm/¾-inch wide strips. Cut the tentacles in half and add to the squid strips.

Preheat a grill pan/skillet over a medium-high heat. Sear the squid and the tentacles for 1–2 minutes until curled up and slightly charred. Remove the pan from the heat and dress with 2 tablespoons of the herb lime dressing.

Layer the chicory, spinach, sliced roast peppers and edamame on a platter. Drizzle with the remaining dressing, and gently mix through. Place the grilled squid on top and garnish with the coriander/cilantro. Serve immediately.

Papaya salad WITH SQUID

Young, unripened papaya is a basic salad ingredient in street food stalls in Thailand, where it is pounded with fresh, spicy ingredients into a cold dish to accompany others. Now this staple dish has found great popularity in the West as the basis of a cold salad mixed with seafood such as crab, lobster, prawns/shrimp or squid.

500 g/18 oz. squid, cleaned, with tentacles separated
4 garlic cloves, peeled
3–4 small fresh red or green chillies/chiles
4 Chinese long beans or 12 green beans, chopped into 5-cm/2-inch lengths
500 g/18 oz. fresh green papaya, peeled, deseeded and cut into fine slivers

2 tomatoes, cut into wedges
4 tablespoons Thai fish sauce
2 tablespoons sugar
4 tablespoons lime juice

TO SERVE
a selection of fresh firm green vegetables in season, such as iceberg lettuce, cucumber or white cabbage
lime wedges

SERVES 4

To prepare the squid tubes, slit down both sides of the tubes and open out. Put on a board soft side up, then lightly run your knife diagonally, both ways, without cutting all the way through, making diamond patterns. The squid will then cook evenly and curl up attractively. Alternatively, just cut the tubes into slices.

Put 600 ml/2½ cups water in a saucepan, bring to the boil, add the squid and simmer for 3 minutes, drain and set aside. Using a large mortar and pestle, pound the garlic to a paste, then add the chillies/chiles and pound again. Add the long beans, breaking them up slightly. Stir in the papaya with a spoon. Lightly pound together, then stir in the tomatoes and lightly pound again. Add the squid and mix well.

Add the fish sauce, sugar and lime juice, stirring well, then transfer to a serving dish. Serve with fresh raw vegetables and lime wedges, using any leaves as a scoop for the spicy mixture.

Vermicelli salad

This light, fresh vermicelli salad is perfect for a light lunch on a sunny day.

125 g/4½ oz. minced/ground pork
10 raw prawns/shrimp, shelled, deveined and coarsely chopped
½ packet (130 g/5 oz.) thin rice vermicelli noodles
10 large dried black fungus mushrooms, soaked for about 10 minutes in cold water until soft, then coarsely chopped

1 large celery stalk, finely sliced
2 tablespoons Thai fish sauce
1 tablespoon sugar
3 tablespoons lime juice
6 small red chillies/chiles, finely chopped
6 spring onions/scallions, thinly sliced
coriander/cilantro leaves, to serve

SERVES 4

Heat 3 tablespoons water in a saucepan, add the minced/ground pork and prawns/shrimp and stir well until the meat is just cooked through.

Then add the noodles, mushrooms, celery, fish sauce, sugar, lime juice, chillies/chiles and spring onions/scallions.

Stir well, transfer to a serving platter and top with coriander/cilantro leaves.

Notes Vermicelli noodles are always sold dried, but are already cooked. Soak in cold water until soft, then chop coarsely. If the dried black fungus mushrooms are very large, they may have a small hard piece in the middle, which should be cut out and discarded.

Asian chicken noodle salad

A seriously addictive and healthy salad that makes a perfect dinner on a warm summer evening. If you don't have time to poach the chicken yourself, shred the meat from a store-bought barbecue chicken or a Peking duck from Chinatown.

400 ml/1²/₃ cups coconut milk

freshly squeezed juice and grated zest of 1 lime

700 g/1½ lbs. (about 5) chicken breasts

1 tablespoon palm sugar

500 g/18 oz. vermicelli glass noodles

100 g/1¾ cups beansprouts

30 g/generous ½ cup coriander/cilantro, chopped

30 g/generous ½ cup fresh mint, chopped

2 carrots, cut into matchsticks

1 cucumber, halved, deseeded and cut into matchsticks

4 spring onions/scallions, finely sliced

1 long red chilli/chile deseeded and cut into thin strips

50 g/½ cup peanuts, toasted (optional)

75 g/¾ cup fried crispy shallots (optional)

DRESSING

1 fresh red chilli/chile, deseeded and finely chopped

1 garlic clove, crushed

4 tablespoons fish sauce

2 tablespoons palm sugar

2 tablespoons freshly squeezed lime juice

2 teaspoons soy sauce

SERVES 6

Begin by poaching the chicken. Combine the coconut milk, lime juice and zest in a saucepan or pot big enough to hold the chicken breasts in one layer. Set over a medium heat, until bubbles start to appear on the surface. Add the chicken to the pan and bring to the boil. Immediately reduce the heat and gently simmer for about 10 minutes, until the chicken is just cooked.

Lift the chicken breasts out of the pan using a slotted spoon and place on a baking sheet to cool. Set the poaching liquid to one side.

To make the dressing, pound the chilli/chile and garlic to a paste in a pestle and mortar. Add the remaining ingredients, mix then set aside.

Place the noodles in a bowl and cover with boiling hot water. Set aside to soak for about 15 minutes.

When the chicken is cool, shred the meat finely and add 60 ml/¼ cup of the reserved poaching liquid to keep it moist.

Drain the noodles using a colander and place in a large serving bowl. Add the shredded chicken, beansprouts, coriander/cilantro, mint, carrot, cucumber, spring onions/scallions and chilli/chile. Pour over a little of the dressing and use your hands to mix everything together.

Top the salad with the toasted nuts and fried shallots, if desired, and serve with the remaining dressing on the side.

Spinach & ricotta dip
WITH FLATBREADS

So quick to whip up and so full of flavour.

a small handful of spinach,
   chopped
a small handful of
   rocket/arugula, chopped
2 spring onions/scallions,
   finely chopped
½ garlic clove, crushed
250 g/1 cup ricotta
6 tablespoons yogurt
2 tablespoons olive oil

2 sprigs of parsley,
   roughly chopped
2 sprigs of dill, roughly chopped
2 tablespoons pesto
chilli/chili oil, to drizzle
sea salt and freshly ground
   black pepper
flatbreads, to serve

SERVES 6

In a bowl mix the spinach, rocket/arugula, spring
onions/scallions, garlic, ricotta, yogurt, salt and pepper
and olive oil. Swirl the herbs and pesto through and
drizzle with chilli/chili oil. Serve with flatbreads.

Sweet potato, smoked mackerel & grapefruit salad

*An amazing combination of ingredients, the
umami comes from the sweet potato and the
smoked mackerel. The grapefruit and fennel add
an important and transformative tangy crunch.*

4 medium sweet potatoes,
   washed and cut into large
   diced pieces
8 garlic cloves, crushed by hand
8 fresh thyme sprigs
4 tablespoons olive oil
sea salt and freshly ground
   black pepper
4 smoked mackerel fillets,

flaked into bite-sized chunks
4 fennel bulbs, thinly sliced
2 pink grapefruit, divided into
   segments and peeled
1 handful chopped flat-leaf
   parsley
2 tablespoons red wine vinegar
4 tablespoons olive oil

SERVES 4

Preheat the oven to 180°C (350°F) Gas 4.

Place the sweet potatoes, garlic and thyme onto
a roasting pan. Drizzle with the olive oil and season
with salt and pepper. Toss to combine and roast for
20–25 minutes. Leave to cool.

Place the mackerel, fennel, grapefruit segments,
cooked sweet potatoes and parsley into a large
mixing bowl. Drizzle with the red wine vinegar and
olive oil and season with salt and pepper.

Toss to combine and serve. This salad is delicious
served with some horseradish cream on the side.

Beer-battered avocado dippers

When it comes to using avocados in cooking, deep-frying is not what immediately springs to mind. However, this is one of those healthy/naughty treats! Take something super-healthy and then deep-fry it in a beer batter... what's not to love? The combination of the crispy batter and the soft avocado centre is amazing, even before you dip it into the creamy chipotle mayo.

6–8 ripe avocados
vegetable oil, for deep-frying

FOR THE BATTER
165 g/1⅓ cups self-raising/rising flour
1 teaspoon salt
1 teaspoon cumin
1 teaspoon dried oregano
1½ teaspoons paprika
½ teaspoon freshly ground black pepper
1 teaspoon ground avocado leaf powder
   (optional)
1 teaspoon baking powder
1 bottle (330 ml/11 fl oz.) Sol beer,
   or substitute your lager of choice

FOR THE CHIPOTLE MAYONNAISE
150 g/¾ cup mayonnaise
2 teaspoons chipotle paste
1 garlic clove, peeled

SERVES 6–8

For the batter, mix together all the dry ingredients until they are well combined. Gently stir in the beer until you have a smooth batter and then put to one side.

For the chipotle mayonnaise, put all the ingredients in a blender and blend for about 1 minute until smooth. Set aside until ready to serve.

Cut the avocados in half, peel them and remove the stones. Slice each half into 3–4 pieces lengthwise, depending on their size.

Pour enough oil into a medium saucepan to reach halfway up the side and heat until hot but not smoking.

Working with one avocado at a time, dip the slices in the batter until well covered, then carefully lower into the oil – it's best to use a slotted spoon to do this to avoid spitting oil.

Fry each batch for about 1 minute so that the batter is golden coloured, but no darker, and crispy. Remove the slices with a slotted spoon and place on a plate lined with paper towels to soak up any excess oil. Repeat with the remaining avocado slices.

Transfer the chipotle mayonnaise to a serving bowl and place on a large serving plate. Arrange the avocado slices on the plate, serve and watch your friends' amazement when they try this dish!

ALL-DAY DINING

Grilled halloumi WITH JALAPEÑO, LIME & TEQUILA RELISH

Halloumi is perfect for grilling/broiling and pan frying. It has a mild taste so it works very well alongside strong flavours or sweet fruits, such as watermelon and figs.

450 g/1 lb. halloumi cheese,
   cut into 5 mm/¼ inch pieces
3 tablespoons olive oil
grated zest and juice of 2 limes
cracked black pepper
extra limes, for squeezing

FOR THE BLISTERED
JALAPEÑO, LIME &
TEQUILA RELISH
3 tablespoons olive oil,
   plus extra for oiling
4 jalapeño chilles/chiles

1 red and 1 white onion,
   thinly sliced
3 garlic cloves, finely chopped
skin of 1 Pickled Kaffir Lime
   (see page 66), finely diced
2 tablespoons tequila
3 tablespoons clear honey
60 ml/¼ cup white wine vinegar
sea salt

SERVES 6

Put a cast-iron pan over medium-high heat and pour in the olive oil. Swirl the pan to coat. Working in batches, add the halloumi and sauté on each side for 2 minutes. Add a little lime zest and juice to the pan per batch.

Put a lightly-oiled cast-iron pan over a high heat until smoking. Add the jalapeños, lower the heat slightly, and cook until the skins are charred and blistered. Remove from the pan and set aside to cool.

Add the oil, sliced onions, and garlic to the pan and cook over medium heat for 5 minutes, stirring occasionally. Season with salt to taste. Add the diced lime skin with the onion.

Roughly chop the cooled jalapeños and add to the pan along with the tequila, honey and vinegar. Cook for a further ten minutes until the onions are golden brown and soft.

Transfer the cheese to a warm serving platter.

Place a teaspoon of relish on top of each piece of cheese. Sprinkle with cracked black pepper and finish with an extra squeeze of lime. Serve.

Crab WITH MANGO & COCONUT

Crab is a wonderful vehicle for other ingredients, which is perfect for this salad, as it is packed full of punchy Thai flavours – coriander/cilantro, fish sauce, lime and chilli/chile. The mango and coconut give it a subtle sweetness and makes this the ideal dish for a barbecue party or an alfresco lunch.

30 g/¼ cup cashews
2 garlic cloves
thumb-size piece of fresh ginger,
   peeled and chopped
2 sweet chillies/chiles, seeded
1 tablespoon nam pla fish sauce
3 teaspoons coconut palm sugar
2 limes (juice of ½ lime and the rest
   cut into wedges for serving)
300 g/10½ oz. crab meat,
   picked through for shells
1 firm, slightly under-ripe mango,
   peeled, pitted and cut into fine strips
handful of fresh coriander/
   cilantro leaves
2 spring onions/scallions, sliced
   on the diagonal
a few radicchio leaves
extra virgin olive oil
½ lemon
sea salt
2 tablespoons shaved or desiccated/
   dried shredded coconut

SERVES 4

Preheat the oven to 180°C (350°F) Gas 4.

Roast the cashews on a baking sheet in the preheated oven for about 10 minutes or until they begin to colour. Watch carefully, as they burn alarmingly quickly!

Using a pestle and mortar, pound the garlic, ginger and chillies/chiles (keeping ½ chilli/chile aside for serving) until you get a paste. Add the fish sauce, coconut sugar and lime juice. Combine until well blended.

Squeeze any excess liquid out of the picked crab. In a large bowl, combine the crab, mango, coriander/cilantro (leaving some aside for serving), spring onions/scallions and roasted cashews. Add the sauce and mix gently.

Dress the radicchio leaves with a little oil, a squeeze of lemon juice and a pinch of salt. Pile the crab mixture on top of the leaves and finish off with the coconut and reserved coriander/cilantro and chilli/chile, sliced. Serve with lime wedges.

Tempura vegetables and shrimp

WITH WASABI MAYONNAISE

This is a wheat-free version of the classic Japanese street food snack, tempura, made using rice and cornflour/cornstarch. You can batter, fry and serve up pretty much any vegetable you like!

selection of vegetables, such as carrot, sweet potato, aubergine/eggplant, squash, broccoli, (bell) pepper, spring onion/scallion, beet(root)

600 ml/2½ cups vegetable, sunflower or rapeseed oil

4 king prawns/jumbo shrimp, shells and central veins removed, but tails on

100 g/¾ cup rice flour, plus extra for coating

100 g/¾ cup cornflour/cornstarch

1 teaspoon baking powder

small bottle of ice-cold sparkling water

2 egg whites

few cubes of ice

sea salt and freshly ground black pepper

mayonnaise mixed with 3 teaspoons wasabi powder or paste, to serve

SERVES 4

Cut the hard vegetables into thin slices about 5 mm/¼ inch thick. Cut softer vegetables like aubergine/eggplant, spring onion/scallion or (bell) pepper a little thicker.

If you have a deep fat fryer, heat the oil to 190°C/375°F, otherwise heat it in a deep saucepan. If you don't have a cooking thermometer, check the temperature by dropping a breadcrumb into the oil. It should turn golden in about 25–30 seconds. Any faster than this and the tempura will burn before the vegetable inside is cooked through.

While the oil is heating, mix together the flours, baking powder, ½ teaspoon salt and a good pinch of pepper in a bowl. Slowly stir in just enough cold sparkling water until you have a yogurt consistency, but don't over-whisk. It doesn't matter if the batter is lumpy; traditionally Japanese tempura batter is not mixed too thoroughly, as the lumps in the batter help to form a more crunchy tempura. Using an electric whisk, beat the egg whites in a separate bowl until they form hard peaks. Fold the eggs into the batter, stir the ice cubes through to keep it as cold as possible.

Lightly coat the vegetables and prawns/shrimp in rice flour. Shake off any excess, then dip into the batter. Carefully place them into the hot oil. Don't overcrowd the fryer or pan, as it will bring down the temperature of the oil. The prawns/shrimp will take about 3 minutes and the vegetables about 2 minutes. Remove all the tempura with a slotted spoon and drain on kitchen paper/paper towels. Serve with the wasabi mayonnaise.

Charred shrimp WITH NAM JIM

This is such a simple yet effective dish and is great for diving into and getting your hands dirty with a big group of friends. The Nam Jim is a wonderfully vibrant Thai sauce that makes these totally addictive. Make sure you use the roots of the coriander/cilantro and not the leaves, as this is where all the flavour is.

roots of 1 bunch of coriander/cilantro
2 garlic cloves
2.5-cm/1-inch piece of fresh ginger
1 large red chilli/chiles, seeded,
    plus extra slices, to serve
1 tablespoon coconut palm sugar
sea salt
2 teaspoons fish sauce
juice of 1 lime
8 king prawns/jumbo shrimp, shell on

SERVES 3–4

Using a pestle and mortar, pound the coriander/cilantro roots, garlic, ginger and chilli/chile until you get a paste. This will take a few minutes of fairly aggressive pounding! The skin of the chilli/chile will also come loose so when that happens, you should pick it out and discard it.

Add the sugar and pound, then add a little salt, the fish sauce and lime juice. Mix together and taste. This Nam Jim is so full of flavour that it should almost sing out at you, with each ingredient holding its own. Adjust it ever so slightly until you get the right balance.

Heat a stovetop grill pan over high heat. Cut the prawns/shrimp lengthways down the middle of the belly, so you have nice long halves. Place them, flesh side down, on the dry pan, cook for 2 minutes, then flip them over and cook for another 2 minutes.

Once cooked, tangle the prawns/shrimp together on a plate with some coriander/cilantro leaves and extra chilli/chile slices scattered over. Drizzle with Nam Jim and serve.

West coast crab cakes

Crab cakes are best when using fresh crab meat. If it is not in season, buy good-quality canned crab meat. Pickled Kaffir Limes (see below) spice up the cakes and make them an enjoyable feast. Serve with herbed yogurt and citrus wedges for extra zing.

450 g/1 lb. fresh crab meat
grated zest and freshly
   squeezed juice of 1 lemon
180 g/³⁄₄ cup fresh corn kernels
2 spring onions/scallions,
   finely chopped
1 egg, lightly beaten
1 jalapeño chilli/chile,
   finely chopped
1½ tablespoons Pickled
   Kaffir Limes (see below)
   finely chopped
sea salt and cracked
   black pepper, to taste
vegetable oil, for frying

COATING
1 egg, lightly beaten
80 g/2 cups fresh or Panko
   breadcrumbs

TO SERVE
fresh lime wedges
natural set yogurt
fresh green herbs, chopped

**MAKES
APPROXIMATELY 12**

Mix together the crab meat, lemon zest and juice, corn, spring onions/scallions, egg, chilli/chile and Pickled Kaffir Limes in a large mixing bowl. Season with salt and pepper.

For the coating, put the egg in a small, shallow bowl and the breadcrumbs on a plate. Shape a large tablespoon of the crab mixture into cakes with your hands. Dip each crab cake into the egg, then roll in the breadcrumbs.

Heat a frying pan/skillet over medium-high heat and drizzle with a little vegetable oil. Working in batches, sauté the crab cakes for 4 minutes on each side until golden brown, crispy and cooked through. Transfer to a warm serving platter and serve with a squeeze of fresh lime and thick, creamy natural yogurt sprinkled with chopped green herbs.

PICKLED KAFFIR LIMES

Keep the pickling solution simple, as you want the wonderful floral aroma of the kaffir limes and leaves to sing. Add to crab cakes, pad Thai, and anything you can think of – they are absolutely delicious!

24 small kaffir limes, quartered
12 kaffir lime leaves
475 ml/2 cups rice wine vinegar
2 tablespoons granulated/
   caster sugar

1 tablespoon rock/kosher salt
*still-warm sterilized glass jars
   with airtight lids*

MAKES 1.8 L/8 CUPS

Pack the limes into warm, sterilized, size-appropriate glass jars, leaving a 1-cm/½-inch space at the top. Divide the kaffir leaves evenly between the jars.

Put the vinegar, sugar and salt in a non-reactive pan and bring to a boil. Reduce the heat and simmer for 5 minutes until the sugar has dissolved.

Pour the hot vinegar mixture over the limes and carefully tap the jars on the counter to get rid of any air pockets. Wipe the jars clean and tightly screw on the lids. Turn the jars upside down to seal. Leave to cool completely, then store in the refrigerator for up to 12 months.

Steamed rice noodle dumplings WITH SCALLOPS

Dim sum or 'yum cha', is always an all-day favourite – bamboo steamers full of small, bite-size dumplings and other delights.

250 g/½ lb. scallops
  (without corals)
50 g/1½ oz. (about 6) water
  chestnuts, drained and
  chopped
2 garlic cloves, crushed
1 tablespoon freshly chopped
  garlic chives
1 tablespoon light soy sauce
2 teaspoons oyster sauce
1 teaspoon sesame oil

24 wonton wrappers
3–4 tablespoons sunflower oil
Szechuan Chilli Dressing
  (see below)
spring onions/scallions,
  thinly sliced to garnish
*a baking sheet lined with
  baking parchment*
a medium bamboo steamer

SERVES 4

Begin by preparing the scallops, cutting away the grey muscle attached at one side and chop into small cubes. Put the scallop meat into a bowl with the chestnuts, garlic, garlic chives, soy sauce, oyster sauce and sesame oil, and stir.

Lay the wonton wrappers flat on a board and place a teaspoon of the scallop mixture in the centre. Brush around the edges with a little water and draw the sides up and around the filling, pressing the edges together to seal. Transfer each one to the prepared baking sheet.

Dip the base of each dumpling in sunflower oil and transfer to the bamboo steamer. Cover and steam over a pan of simmering water for 10–12 minutes until firm and cooked through.

Serve with the dressing, garnished with shredded spring onions/scallions.

SZECHUAN CHILLI DRESSING

The perfect sauce for dipping hot steamed and fried dumplings into.

100 ml/⅓ cup sunflower oil
1–2 teaspoons dried red chilli/
  hot red pepper flakes
2 tablespoons light soy sauce
1 tablespoon black vinegar

2 teaspoons caster/
  granulated sugar
¼ teaspoon Szechuan
  peppercorns

MAKES 200 ML/¾ CUP

Heat the oil in a small saucepan set over a medium heat until it just starts to shimmer. Remove from the heat and stir in the chilli/hot red pepper flakes. Set aside for 30 minutes, then strain through a fine mesh sieve/strainer into a clean bowl. Stir in the remaining ingredients and serve as required.

Tip If you are making this dressing ahead of time omit the peppercorns and add just before serving.

Mee grob

Sometimes called 'mee krob', this crispy noodle dish is a popular Thai dish. Be careful when deep-frying noodles as the oil bubbles up quite dramatically.

100 g/3½ oz. dried rice vermicelli
  noodles
2 eggs, beaten
125 g/1 cup firm tofu, cubed
1 tablespoon dried shrimp
1 Asian shallot, thinly sliced
1 tablespoon pickled garlic
50 g/1 cup beansprouts, trimmed
a small bunch of fresh coriander/cilantro
6 garlic chives, roughly chopped
vegetable oil, for deep-frying

SAUCE
125 g/½ cup plus 1 tablespoon grated
  palm sugar
1 tablespoon yellow bean sauce
2 tablespoons fish sauce
1 tablespoon freshly squeezed lime juice

SERVES 4

Put the noodles in a bowl, cover with boiling water and soak for 20 minutes until softened. Drain the noodles and pat dry with paper towels.

Next make the sauce. Put the palm sugar in a saucepan with 1 tablespoon cold water set over a low heat. Heat gently, stirring continuously, until the sugar dissolves. Turn up the heat and boil for a minute until the syrup turns lightly golden, then stir in the yellow bean paste, fish sauce and lime juice. Simmer gently for 3–4 minutes until thick and keep warm until ready to use.

Pour vegetable oil into a wok or large saucepan to reach about 5 cm/2 inches up the side and set over a medium-high heat. Heat until a cube of bread dropped into the oil crisps in 30 seconds. Add the noodles in small bunches and fry for 1–2 minutes until crisp and golden. Remove with a slotted spoon and drain on paper towels. Repeat with the remaining noodles until you have fried them all. Keep the pan on the heat.

Break the noodles into a large mixing bowl and set aside.

Strain the beaten egg through a fine mesh sieve/strainer and pour half into the hot oil – it will puff up into a lacy cake. Fry for 30 seconds, flip over and fry for a further 30 seconds until crisp and brown, then remove with a slotted spoon. Drain on paper towels and repeat with the remaining egg.

Deep-fry the tofu and set aside.

Deep-fry the dried shrimp for 10 seconds and remove with a slotted spoon.

Carefully discard all but 1 tablespoon of the oil and stir-fry the shallot and garlic for 5 minutes until lightly crisp. Stir in the beansprouts and remove the pan from the heat. Add all the fried ingredients along with the coriander/cilantro and garlic chives to the noodles and stir to combine. Pour in the sauce, stir again and serve at once.

Spicy peanut noodles

These noodles are cloaked in a wonderful spicy peanut sauce which can be served either ice cold or warm. They make a great summer dish on their own, but are even better served with something caramelized and charred, hot off the grill. Keep the leftover sauce in a glass jar with a lid in the fridge and add a spoonful to dressings or mix into rice.

250-g/9-oz. packet of
  buckwheat soba noodles
80 g/⅓ cup Doenjang
  (Korean bean paste)
80 g/⅓ cup Gochujang
  (Korean chilli/chile paste)
coriander/cilantro, chopped,
  to garnish
sesame seeds, to garnish
4 limes, quartered
Cucumber Pickles (see below)

FOR THE SAUCE
2 tablespoons dark honey
2 tablespoons toasted sesame oil
½ yellow onion, roughly
  chopped
3 spring onions/scallions,
  roughly chopped
2 tablespoons peanut butter
2 tablespoons rice wine vinegar
salt and freshly ground
  black pepper

SERVES 4
sauce yields 250 ml/1 cup

Cook the soba noodles according to the packet instructions. Rinse under cold water and set aside.

To make the sauce, place the honey, sesame oil, onion, spring onions/scallions, peanut butter and vinegar in a blender and process until smooth. Season with salt and pepper.

Place the noodles in a large bowl and spoon over 2–3 tablespoons of the sauce. Toss together, making sure the noodles are well coated in the sauce. Sprinkle with coriander/cilantro and sesame seeds. Serve the limes on the side for squeezing over, along with the Cucumber Pickles.

CUCUMBER PICKLES

6 Persian cucumbers,
  sliced into rounds
2 bay leaves
500 ml/2 cups white wine
  vinegar
110 g/½ cup white sugar

2 tablespoons kosher salt
2 teaspoons mustard seeds
sterilized glass jar with an
  airtight lid

SERVES 4

Make the pickles ahead of time as they will need to marinate for at least an hour.

Pack the cucumbers and bay leaves into a sterilized glass jar. Bring the vinegar, sugar, salt, mustard seeds and 60 ml/¼ cup water to the boil in a saucepan over a medium-high heat. Reduce to a simmer and cook for 5 minutes until the sugar has dissolved. Pour the hot mixture over the cucumbers, cap with a tight-fitting lid, and set aside. These will keep for up to 6 months in the fridge.

Tofu steaks WITH SESAME & SOY DRESSING

This recipe for a delicious yet simple meatless meal has substantial texture and satisfying flavour. Tofu comes in several different firmnesses, making it a super versatile ingredient to cook with. It is a great source of protein and calcium and is low in calories. The sesame and soy dressing adds umami richness to the dish.

800 g/1¾ lb. firm tofu, drained
80 g/2¾ oz. shio koji (or 1 teaspoon sea salt)
50 g/1¾ oz. katakuriko (potato starch) or cornflour/cornstarch
2 tablespoons vegetable oil

SESAME & SOY DRESSING
2 tablespoons toasted sesame oil
2 tablespoons vegetable oil
2 tablespoons flaked/slivered almonds
2 garlic cloves, thinly sliced
20 g/¾ oz. fresh ginger, peeled and finely chopped
2 spring onions/scallions, thinly sliced
3 tablespoons soy sauce
2 tablespoons mirin
2 tablespoons toasted white sesame seeds
1 tablespoon dried goji berries
sea salt
2 red radishes, cut into matchsticks, to serve
mixed leaf salad, to serve

SERVES 4

If you are using shio koji, slice the tofu into four 'steaks'. Rub the surface of the tofu with the shio koji and place in a resealable plastic bag, squeezing out any air. Refrigerate and leave to marinate for a minimum of 20 minutes or overnight. The shio koji will draw out excess moisture.

If you are using sea salt instead of shio koji, wrap the tofu in plenty of kitchen paper/paper towels and compress under a heavy kitchen utensil for 30 minutes to remove excess water.

Slice the tofu into four 'steaks'. Rub the surface of the tofu with the salt to season and skip the marinating step.

To make the sesame and soy dressing, combine the toasted sesame oil and vegetable oil in a saucepan over a medium heat. When it becomes hot (but not smoking), fry the almonds and garlic, stirring regularly, until pale golden in colour. Take care that they don't burn.

Turn the heat off and transfer the almonds and garlic to kitchen paper/paper towels to drain off any excess oil.

Add the ginger and spring onions/scallions to the oil in the pan while it is still hot and let them sizzle in the residual heat as the oil cools.

Once the oil has cooled down, stir in the soy sauce, mirin, toasted sesame seeds and goji berries. Season the oil with a little sea salt.

Wipe the tofu 'steaks' with kitchen paper/paper towels to remove any excess moisture or shio koji. Lightly coat the tofu 'steaks' in the katakuriko (potato starch) or cornflour/cornstarch. Place the vegetable oil in a frying pan/skillet over a medium heat and fry the tofu slices for 1–2 minutes on each side until crisp.

Pour the sesame and soy dressing over the tofu 'steaks' to serve and garnish with the fried almonds and garlic and sliced radishes. Serve with mixed leaf salad.

Sticky aubergine poke

WITH SOUR CARROT SALAD

This is a poke take on the traditional Japanese favourite, Nasu Denganku, and pays homage to Hawaiian and Japanese fusion cooking.

900 g/2 lb. aubergines/eggplants
4 shallots
125 g/⅔ cup demerara/turbinado sugar
2 garlic cloves, crushed
1½ teaspoons crushed green
    peppercorns
75 ml/5 tablespoons soy sauce
small handful of kale, chopped
small handful of coriander/cilantro,
    chopped

FOR THE SUSHI RICE
250 g/1½ cups sushi rice
1 teaspoon salt
2 tablespoons white sugar
3 tablespoons rice vinegar
2 tablespoons mirin

FOR THE SOUR
CARROT SALAD
3 spring onions/scallions, finely sliced
    diagonally into long strands
200 g/1½ cups finely grated carrots
1 tablespoon demerara/turbinado sugar
¼ teaspoon salt
1 tablespoon boiling water
freshly squeezed juice of 1 large lime
1 teaspoon rice wine vinegar

SERVES 4 AS AN APPETIZER

First make the carrot salad. Mix the grated carrots and spring onions/scallions in a bowl. Dissolve the sugar and salt in the boiling water. Stir in the lime juice and vinegar and add this dressing to the carrot and onion mix. Set aside.

Prepare the sushi rice. Rinse the rice at least three times in cold water. Place in a medium-sized pan with 500 ml/2 cups water and bring to the boil. Reduce the heat to a low simmer and cover with a lid. The rice should absorb all the water and be tender after 20 minutes. Meanwhile, combine the salt, sugar, rice vinegar and mirin in a bowl. Tip the rice out of the pan onto a metal tray and spread out so that it cools quickly. Gently pour over the vinegar mixture and combine by running through the rice with a fork. Cover with clingfilm/plastic wrap if not using immediately (the cooked rice should be used within a day).

Cut the aubergines/eggplants into 2.5-cm/1-inch cubes. Finely slice the shallots. Have them both at hand when you are making the caramel as you will have to act quickly.

Put the sugar in a large wok set over a high heat. Swirl the wok to help melt the sugar. The sugar will have a lovely amber tone. After about 5 minutes it will start to caramelize at the edges. Swirl the wok once more to distribute the caramel evenly, then add the aubergines/eggplants and shallots. Toss until the chunks are well coated, then cook for 2 minutes. Lower the heat, add the garlic and green peppercorns and cook for 2 minutes. Add the soy sauce and simmer, loosely covered with foil, for 7 minutes or until the sauce reduces to a thick consistency. To serve, divide the carrot salad, aubergine/eggplant mixture, kale and rice between four bowls, scatter over the coriander/cilantro.

'Ahi katsu

'Ahi katsu is a popular dish in Hawai'i. This version is slightly fancier than the original local favourite, with an added layer of nori seaweed to give that extra umami element, but the recipe can just as easily be made without the nori and with pork, chicken, squid or another fish (such as mahi mahi/dorado or even cod or halibut) instead of the 'ahi.

900 g/2 lb. 'ahi or yellowfin tuna fillets
1 tablespoon salt
1 tablespoon freshly ground black pepper
130 g/1 cup plain/all-purpose flour
4 eggs
100 g/2 cups panko breadcrumbs
8 sheets of nori seaweed
vegetable oil, for frying

FOR THE SAUCE
100 ml/⅓ cup light shoyu sauce
2 tablespoons dry mustard, mixed
    with a little water to make a paste
225 g/1 cup mayonnaise

TO SERVE
steamed white rice
furikake seasoning

SERVES 12

Cut the fish into slices roughly 18 cm/7 inches long and 2.5 cm/1 inch thick.

You will need three wide, shallow bowls. In the first bowl, mix the salt, pepper and flour. Break the eggs into the second bowl and beat them with a fork. Put all the panko breadcrumbs into the third bowl.

Wrap each fillet of fish in a sheet of nori so the seaweed overlaps. Lightly wet the tip of your finger in water and run it along the edge of the nori to help it stick and stay wrapped around the 'ahi. Dip each fillet into the flour mixture, then in the egg wash and finally coat with the panko breadcrumbs.

Shallow-fry the breadcrumbed fillets in vegetable oil over a medium heat, for 2–3 minutes on each side, turning frequently until evenly browned and golden. Place on a plate covered in paper towels to drain away the excess oil, then slice.

For the sauce, mix together the shoyu, mustard paste and mayonnaise and serve as a side sauce, along with some steamed white rice and furikake.

Kaffir lime, squid & noodle salad

This dish can be found in many guises originating from Thailand, Vietnam and Laos, as well as Cambodia. The squid is tenderized with a little salt, sugar and lime juice and then grilled on skewers over hot coals or in a grill pan.

150 g/5 oz. dried cellophane noodles
500 g/1 lb. cleaned squid
½ teaspoon salt
½ teaspoon caster/granulated sugar
1 tablespoon freshly squeezed lime juice
2 snake beans or green beans, trimmed and very thinly sliced
1 long red chilli/chile, deseeded and thinly sliced
2 red Asian shallots, thinly sliced
2 kaffir lime leaves, very thinly sliced
1 lemon grass stalk, trimmed and very thinly sliced
a small handful each of fresh mint, coriander/cilantro and Thai basil leaves

DEEP-FRIED SHALLOTS
12 Asian shallots, thinly sliced
vegetable oil, for deep-frying

DRESSING
1 tablespoon freshly squeezed lime juice
1 teaspoon coriander/cilantro paste
2–3 teaspoons fish sauce
1–2 teaspoons caster/granulated sugar
6–8 bamboo skewers, soaked in cold water for 30 minutes

SERVES 4

Soak the noodles in a bowlful of hot water for 30 minutes until softened. Drain well with a clean kitchen cloth and set aside in a large mixing bowl.

To make the dressing, combine all the ingredients together in a small bowl and stir well to dissolve the sugar.

Next prepare the squid. Cut the cleaned squid bodies in half and score the inside of the flesh with a sharp knife to make a diamond pattern. Cut into 5-cm/2-inch pieces. Put the squid in a large mixing bowl and add the salt, sugar and lime juice, and rub well into the flesh. Set aside for 10 minutes and then thread the squid onto the pre-soaked skewers and set aside.

Next make the deep-fried shallots. Pour the oil into a wok or (old) saucepan about 5 cm/2 inches up the side of the pan and set over a medium heat. Test the temperature of the pan by dropping a cube of bread into the hot oil – it should be crisp within 30 seconds. Deep-fry the shallots in batches for 2–3 minutes until crisp and golden. Remove with a slotted spoon and drain on kitchen paper/paper towels.

Put the remaining salad ingredients in a separate large mixing bowl, add 1 tablespoon of the dressing and toss well to coat. Add the noodles and toss again to mix.

Preheat a stovetop ridged grill pan over a high heat and when it starts to smoke cook the squid for 1 minute each side until charred. Remove the squid from the skewers and add to the noodles, drizzling the remaining dressing over the top. Toss well to coat and serve immediately, garnished with the deep-fried shallots.

Teriyaki burger

Affectionately known as 'teri burgers', these are an Hawaiian take on an American classic. The teri sauce gives these burgers a sweet, sticky quality and helps to keep the meat moist and extra succulent. These are also great when cooked on the barbecue or grilled/broiled.

450 g/1 lb. minced/ground steak
1 bunch spring onions/scallions, finely sliced (white and green parts)
1 teaspoon finely chopped fresh ginger
1 teaspoon finely chopped garlic
¼ teaspoon freshly ground black pepper
¼ teaspoon sea salt
2½ tablespoons teriyaki sauce
10 g/¼ cup panko breadcrumbs

1 tablespoon toasted sesame seeds
2 tablespoons vegetable oil
4 burger buns, warmed (brioche buns work well)
thinly sliced red onion, lettuce and tomato, to serve
Kalua Chipotle Ketchup (see below)
Cucumber Pickles (see page 74), to serve

MAKES 4

Place the steak in a large bowl with the spring onions/scallions, ginger, garlic, pepper, salt, teriyaki sauce, panko breadcrumbs and sesame seeds. Mix together well. Divide the mixture into four burgers and shape into round patties, approx. 2.5 cm/1 inch thick.

Heat the oil in a heavy-based frying pan/skillet over a medium-high heat. Fry the burgers for approx. 4 minutes on each side, or for a little longer if you prefer your burger well-done.

Serve each burger in a warm bun with thinly sliced red onion, lettuce and tomato. Serve with Kalua Chipotle Ketchup on the side along with some Cucumber Pickles.

Tip For an extra tropical twist, top each of your burgers with a grilled/broiled pineapple ring.

KALUA CHIPOTLE KETCHUP

This Mexican-inspired sauce has everything you want, with heat and a deep smoky undertone, it will transform anything it touches. Also makes a great BBQ marinade.

3 x 400-g/14-oz. cans whole Italian tomatoes
3 tablespoons dark soy sauce
3 tablespoons muscovado sugar
1 teaspoon fish sauce
1 tablespoon mirin

3 tablespoons chipotle paste
sterilized glass bottles with airtight lids (optional)

MAKES 4 X 150-ML/ 5-OZ. BOTTLES

Put the whole tomatoes in a saucepan and heat gently. Add the soy sauce, muscovado sugar, fish sauce and mirin. Stir and bring the mixture to a very low simmer. Add in the chipotle paste and stir together. Continue to simmer for approx. 30 minutes until slightly reduced. Put everything in a blender and whizz to a smooth purée.

Sterilize the bottles by putting them in a boiling water bath, or microwave. When the bottles are ready, pour in the warm sauce and close the seals or lids. Store in a dry place, out of the light. Once open, keep the bottle in the fridge and use within one week.

Pipikaula

The name Pipikaula literally translates as 'beef rope' in Hawaiian. It should be more moist and tender than the usual tough, leathery biltong-style jerky. Typically this dish would be taken to a luau or to the beach and shared around, eaten as a pupu (or snack).

1.8 kg/4 lb. flank steak
sesame seeds and spring
  onions/scallions, finely sliced,
  to garnish

FOR THE MARINADE
235 ml/1 cup soy sauce
120 ml/½ cup sake or dry sherry
2 tablespoons liquid smoke
2 tablespoons brown cane sugar
  (or use brown or demerara/
  turbinado)

2 teaspoons sea salt flakes
¼ teaspoon freshly ground
  black pepper
1 tablespoon finely chopped
  fresh ginger
2 garlic cloves, finely chopped
2 red chillies/chiles, deseeded
  and finely chopped

MAKES APPROX
1.5 KG/3 LB. 5 OZ.

Pound the beef with a mallet or wooden spoon to tenderize. Cutting along the grain, slice the steak into strips approx. 4 cm/1½ inches wide.

Combine the marinade ingredients in a large mixing bowl. Add the meat to the mixing bowl and coat fully in the marinade. Cover and refrigerate for 24 hours, turning the steak slices occasionally to ensure the marinade is well absorbed.

Drain the meat. Discard the marinade.

Place a cooling rack on top of a baking sheet covered in baking parchment. Arrange the meat pieces so they lay flat on the cooling rack.

Dry the meat in the oven at around 80°C (175°F) for 7–8 hours, until the beef gets a 'jerky' texture. If you have a dehydrator or dry box, you can use this instead, although it will take a bit longer (at least two days in a hot sun with the box being brought in at night).

To serve, cut slices diagonally (about 1 cm/½ inch thick) and garnish with sesame seeds and spring onions/scallions. Eat with chopsticks, sharing with friends and enjoying 'pupu' style.

Tip For a more tropical twist, try swapping the soy sauce for 235 ml/1 cup pineapple juice.

The dried meat may be stored in an airtight container in the refrigerator for up to 5 days, or in the freezer, wrapped, for 6–8 months.

Fish tacos WITH CHIPOTLE-LIME CREMA

Here, roasted white fish with a gentle crust of coriander/cilantro and pumpkin seeds is complimented by the addition of guacamole and chipotle-lime crema. It's the taste of summer.

CHIPOTLE-LIME CREMA
1 dried chipotle chilli/chile plus 2 tablespoons just-boiled water (or substitute chipotle powder, or smoked barbecue sauce with cayenne pepper)
4 tablespoons crème fraîche, sour cream or natural/plain yogurt
juice and zest of ½ lime
a few coriander/cilantro leaves

FISH TACOS
700 g/1 lb. 9 oz. skinless white fish fillets (such as sea bass, John Dory, barramundi or mahi-mahi)
2 handfuls coriander/cilantro leaves and stems, chopped
1 handful pumpkin seeds/pepitas
2 tablespoons olive oil
zest of ½ lime

TO SERVE
warmed corn or wheat soft tortillas or tacos (2–3 per person)
Guacamole (see below)
4 large handfuls shredded white cabbage
jalapeños, to taste
salt
stick blender or small food processor

SERVES 4

Split the dried chipotle chilli/chile and shake out most of the seeds. Dry-toast it in a frying pan/skillet until it smells nutty. Cover it with just-boiled water and steep for 15 minutes. Purée the chilli/chile and the steeping water until smooth.

Put 2 teaspoons of the chipotle purée in the bottom of a blender. Add the crème fraîche and lime zest and juice. Process until smooth and top with a few coriander/cilantro leaves.

Preheat the oven to 200°C (400°F) Gas 6.

Dry the fish fillets well and place them on a baking sheet. Cover them with a flurry of coriander/cilantro leaves, pumpkin seeds/pepitas, a drizzle of olive oil and the zest of half a lime (use the juice in the guacamole).

Bake the fish for 10–12 minutes, until the flesh is opaque, or wrap in foil and grill on the barbecue. Break each cooked fillet into thirds (keeping the pumpkin seeds and coriander with each one).

Place the fish on a serving platter with the tortillas, guacamole, shredded cabbage, chipotle-lime crema and jalapeños, and assemble your own tacos.

Any remaining chipotle purée can be frozen in an ice cube tray, so there's some on hand next time you make tacos, burritos, enchiladas or pulled pork.

GUACAMOLE

2 ripe avocados
juice of ½ lime
1 handful coriander/cilantro leaves, roughly chopped
60 g/2 cups good corn chips, warmed in the oven for 10 minutes
6 soft corn tortillas, wrapped in foil and warmed in the oven
salt

SERVES 4

Halve the avocados and cut out any brown bits. Remove the stones/pits. Use a fork to scrape the avocado flesh from the skin.

Mash the avocado flesh with the lime juice, salt and half the coriander/cilantro. Top with the remaining coriander and a sprinkle of salt. Eat with warm corn chips and warm tortillas. For a textural riot, combine the two.

Yuzu lomi lomi salmon poke

This citrus-based sauce really sets this poke apart. Use a combination of orange and lime, if you can't source yuzu.

250 g/1½ cups sushi rice (see right)
1 teaspoon yuzu
2 tablespoons mirin
2 tablespoons light soy sauce
500 g/1 lb. 2 oz. very fresh salmon
3 spring onions/scallions
Yuzu-Mango Salsa (see below), to serve

OPTIONAL TOPPINGS
2 tablespoons edamame
1 teaspoon furikake seasoning
1 tablespoon shredded seaweed
1 teaspoon black sesame seeds
2 tablespoons Pickled Ginger (see below)
edible flowers, to garnish

SERVES 4

Prepare a batch of sushi rice.

Make up the marinade by mixing up the yuzu, mirin and light soy. Cube the salmon and put into a bowl with enough marinade to just provide a glistening surface for the salmon. Add some very finely sliced spring onions/scallions.

Make the poke by spooning some rice into bowls, add some of the salmon, then finish by topping with the edamame beans, furikake, seaweed, black sesame seeds and pickled ginger. To serve, add some Yuzu-Mango Salsa directly on top.

YUZU-MANGO SALSA

2 ripe mangoes, peeled and stoned
3 spring onions/scallions
2 small red chillies/chiles
2 tablespoons yuzu juice
4 tablespoons apple juice

SERVES 4

Cut half into small dice, and put the other half into a blender with the spring onions/scallions, chillies/chiles, and yuzu and apple juices. Blitz until fairly smooth. Mix together with the diced mango.

BASIC SUSHI RICE

250 g/1½ cups sushi rice
1 teaspoon salt
2 tablespoons white sugar
3 tablespoons rice vinegar
2 tablespoons mirin

ENOUGH FOR 4 SERVINGS IN POKE RECIPES

Rinse the rice at least three times in cold water. Place in a medium-sized pan with 500 ml/2 cups water and bring to the boil. After the water reaches boiling point, reduce the heat to a low simmer and cover with a lid. The rice should absorb all the water and be tender after 20 minutes.

Meanwhile, combine the salt, sugar, rice vinegar and mirin in a bowl. Tip the rice out of the pan onto a metal tray and spread out so that it cools quickly. You can aid the cooling process by fanning. While fanning the rice, gently pour over the vinegar mixture and combine by running through the rice with a fork. Cover with clingfilm/plastic wrap if not using immediately (the rice should be used within a day).

PICKLED GINGER

250 g/9 oz. fresh ginger – try using young ginger
1 tablespoon Maldon sea salt
60 g/5 tablespoons sugar
300 ml/1¼ cups rice wine vinegar
3 tablespoons water
sterilized glass jar with an airtight lid

SERVES 4

Peel the ginger and slice thinly. Pile into a bowl and rub in the salt. Cover and refrigerate for at least 2 hours. Squeeze the ginger to remove the salt and the liquid, then place the ginger in the preserving jar.

Bring the remaining ingredients to a simmer in a small pan. Make sure the sugar is dissolved. Pour into the jar and cool a little before sealing.

Leave undisturbed for at least three days before using to allow the flavours to mellow.

Spicy pork burger WITH MANGO SALSA

The spicy Asian flavours and sweet fresh mango salsa set this succulent pork burger apart from a traditional beef burger, and makes a lighter alternative too.

45 ml/3 tablespoons olive oil
115 g/¾ cup (about 1 small) finely diced onion
3 garlic cloves, crushed
a 4-cm/1½-inch piece of ginger, peeled and finely grated
900 g/2 lbs. minced/ground pork
2 long red chillies/chiles, deseeded and finely chopped
1 tablespoon fish sauce
2 tablespoons chopped coriander/cilantro
60 g/2 oz. bacon
2 eggs
sea salt and freshly ground black pepper, to season

MANGO SALSA
2 mangos, peeled, pitted and very finely diced
1 long fresh red chilli/chile, deseeded and finely diced
1 tablespoon chopped coriander/cilantro
1 tablespoon roughly chopped mint leaves
½ medium red onion, finely diced
freshly squeezed juice of 1 lime
2 teaspoons palm sugar

FENNEL & MINT SLAW
2 heaped tablespoons mayonnaise
freshly squeezed juice and grated zest of 1 lemon
200 g/7 oz. (about 1 small) fennel bulb, trimmed and sliced into rings
a bunch of fresh mint
40 g/scant 1 cup flat-leaf parsley
40 g/1½ oz. rocket/arugula
½ red onion, finely sliced

TO SERVE
6 burger buns
mayonnaise

SERVES 6

To make the mango salsa, mix all of the ingredients together in a bowl and set aside.

To make the slaw, mix the mayonnaise with the lemon juice and zest and then dress the fennel straight away to prevent the fennel discolouring. Gently mix through the herbs, rocket/arugula and the red onion.

For the burgers, heat 1 tablespoon of the oil in a frying pan/skillet and sauté the onion, garlic and ginger over a gentle heat until soft. Remove from the heat and allow to cool.

Place the remaining ingredients in a large bowl, add the onion mixture and combine.

Season with salt and pepper.

Form into 6 burger patties (about 180 g/6½ oz. each). Refrigerate until ready to cook. Preheat the oven to 170°C (325°F) Gas 3.

Heat the remaining 2 tablespoons of oil in a large frying pan/skillet and fry the burger patties for 4 minutes, turning once, until nice and brown on both sides. You may need to do this in batches, depending on the size of your pan/skillet.

Transfer the patties to a baking sheet and finish off in the oven for a further 10 minutes.

While the patties are cooking, lightly toast the burger buns. Spread some mayonnaise on the bottom bun and top with the pork pattie, mango salsa and the other half of the bun. Serve with the fennel & mint slaw on the side.

Beef bulgogi and rice noodle wraps

The word bulgogi means 'fire meat' and refers to marinated and grilled meats, usually beef. Here it is stir-fried and combined with shiitake mushrooms and Korean sweet potato noodles, wrapped in lettuce leaves and topped with kimchi and ssamjang.

500 g/1 lb. beef rib-eye steak
2 tablespoons light or dark
   soy sauce
2 tablespoons soft brown sugar
1 Asian shallot, finely chopped
1 garlic clove, crushed
2 teaspoons sesame oil,
   plus extra for dressing
½ teaspoon Chinese five-spice
   powder

125 g/4 oz. sweet potato
   noodles
2 tablespoons peanut oil
125 g/4 oz. shiitake mushrooms,
   trimmed and cut into quarters
4 tablespoons kimchi
Ssamjang Sauce (see right)

SERVES 4

Begin by preparing the beef. Thinly slice the steak and arrange in a single layer in a wide, shallow dish. Combine the soy sauce, sugar, shallot, garlic, sesame oil and Chinese five-spice powder, and pour over the beef. Set aside to marinate for at least 1 hour.

Plunge the sweet potato noodles into a pan of boiling water and cook for 4–5 minutes until al dente.

Drain, refresh under cold water and drain again. Shake the noodles dry and dress with a little sesame oil to prevent them from sticking together. Set aside.

Heat the oil in a wok or large frying pan/skillet set over a medium heat until it starts to shimmer. Add the beef in batches and stir-fry for 2–3 minutes until golden. Remove with a slotted spoon. Add the mushrooms and any remaining marinade and stir-fry for 1 minute. Return the beef to the pan along with the noodles and stir-fry for 1 minute, until everything is heated through.

Divide the beef noodles between bowls and serve with lettuce leaves, kimchi and the ssamjang sauce. Wrap, roll and eat.

SSAMJANG SAUCE

60 ml/4 tablespoons doenjang
2 teaspoons gochujang
1 spring onion/scallion, trimmed
   and finely chopped
1 small garlic clove, crushed
1 Asian shallot, finely chopped

2 teaspoons rice wine
2 teaspoons sesame oil
1 teaspoon clear honey
1 teaspoon sesame seeds,
   toasted

MAKES 150 ML/⅔ CUP

Put all the ingredients in a small bowl and use as required.

Alternatively, transfer to a plastic container, seal and store in the fridge for up to 3 days.

BEACHSIDE BBQ

Grilled market vegetable salad WITH HERBED TOASTS

This recipe can be a combination of anything from tomatoes to squash to celery. Pile the beautifully charred vegetables onto a large wooden board with grilled toasts and serve.

1 head Radicchio Treviso, quartered

1 head Romaine/cos lettuce, quartered

2 small fennel, with fronds, quartered

6 courgettes/zucchini halved

160 g/1 cup cherry tomatoes

6 Japanese aubergines/ eggplants, halved

1 recipe of Spanish Sherry Marinade (see below)

coarse sea salt, to sprinkle

extra virgin olive oil, to drizzle

a handful of freshly torn flat-leaf parsley, to garnish

HERBED TOASTS

1 large baguette, thickly sliced

1 recipe of Garden Herb Butter (see below)

SERVES 6–8

Put all the vegetables in a large ceramic baking dish and pour over the Spanish Sherry Marinade. Toss to cover well and set aside.

Spread a generous amount of Garden Herb Butter on both sides of the baguette slices and set aside.

Heat the barbecue/grill to medium. In batches, grill the vegetables, turning them over, until slightly charred all over. Some vegetables will cook quicker than others so remove these from the barbecue/grill as they are cooked. Transfer the vegetables to a large wooden board and dress lightly with any of the remaining marinade.

Grill the baguette slices until well toasted and place on the board alongside the vegetables. Sprinkle generously with the coarse sea salt, drizzle with olive oil, and garnish with fresh parsley, to serve.

SPANISH SHERRY MARINADE

120 ml/½ cup extra virgin olive oil

60 ml/¼ cup Jerez Spanish vinegar

2 garlic cloves, finely chopped

1 shallot, finely chopped

a pinch of Spanish smoked

paprika (pimentòn)

coarse sea salt and cracked black pepper

sterilized glass jar with airtight lids (optional)

YIELDS SCANT 200 ML/1 CUP

Put all the ingredients in a bowl and mix together.

Store the marinade in a glass jar in the refrigerator for up to 1 month.

GARDEN HERB BUTTER

120 g/1 stick unsalted butter, at room temperature

2 generous tablespoons fresh oregano leaves

2 generous tablespoons fresh marjoram leaves

2 generous tablespoons fresh thyme leaves

1 generous tablespoon fresh rosemary leaves

Sel de Gris and ground black pepper

YIELDS GENEROUS 130 G/½ CUP

Put all the ingredients in a food processor and process until smooth but leaving a little texture in the butter. Refrigerate until ready to use.

To make a butter roll, spoon the butter mixture onto a piece of clingfilm/plastic wrap. Fold the film/wrap over the butter and roll into a sausage shape. Twist the ends to secure and store in the fridge. When you're ready to use the butter, slice off discs as desired.

Mexican grilled corn

oil, for brushing the grate
250 g/1 cup Mexican Crema
    or crème frâiche
255 g/1/2 cup mayonnaise
1 jalapeño, seeded and finely diced
1 tablespoon chilli/chili powder,
    plus extra for garnishing
160 g/1½ cups Cotija cheese (or feta
    cheese, if you cannot find Coteja)
sea salt
6 corn cobs in the husk
3 tablespoons olive oil
small bunch of coriander/cilantro,
    finely chopped
6 lime wedges, quartered

SERVES 6

Grilled corn slathered in cream, cheese and chillies/ chiles and finished off with freshly squeezed limes are known as 'elotes' in Mexico and sold as street food. Use the husk as a handle when eating.

Heat the barbeque/grill to medium-high. Brush the grate with oil.

Place the crema, mayonnaise, jalapeño, chilli/chili powder, and half the cheese in a medium-sized bowl and mix together. Season with salt.

Peel the corn husks back and twist to make a handle. Brush the corn with the olive oil and place on the grill. Cook for about 10–12 minutes, turning every 3–4 minutes, until the corn is golden and caramelized.

When the corn is ready, generously brush the crema mixture over the kernels. Sprinkle with the remaining cheese and coriander/cilantro and finish with a dusting of chilli/chili powder. Serve with the lime wedges to squeeze over.

Spiced red snapper WITH CHARMOULA

Fish cooked over hot coals is a summer classic; reminiscent of fishing and then cooking the catch on the beach. Snapper is an excellent fish to grill with. It's sturdy and the meat just falls off the bones. Always have lots of freshly cut lemons and limes on hand to squeeze over the fish.

4 red snapper
2 lemons, thinly sliced
1 recipe of Charmoula Paste
 (see below)

sea salt and cracked
 black pepper
2 lemons, quartered, to serve
2 limes, quartered, to serve

SERVES 4

Wash the snapper under cold water and pat dry. Lay the fish on a platter big enough to hold them all.

Stuff the snapper with the sliced lemons and brush the fish inside and out with Charmoula Paste. Season with salt and pepper.

Preheat the barbecue/grill or set a grill pan over a medium-high heat.

Lay the fish on the hot barbecue/grill and cook for 8–10 minutes on each side, depending on the thickness of the fish, until the flesh is cooked through. Remove the fish from the barbecue/grill or grill pan, cover with foil and let rest for 5 minutes.

Serve the fish with lemon and lime quarters.

CHARMOULA PASTE

Charmoula is a wonderful mixture of north African-inspired spices with a good pinch of saffron and never ceases to disappoint.

1 tablespoon ground coriander
1 tablespoon ground cumin
4 garlic cloves, finely chopped
a large bunch of fresh flat-leaf
 parsley, finely chopped
1 teaspoon dried chilli/chili flakes
1/2 teaspoon smoked paprika
a good pinch saffron threads

2 tablespoons freshly
 squeezed lime juice
120 ml/1/2 cup olive oil
*sterilized glass jar with
 airtight lids (optional)*

YIELDS 360 ML/
1 1/2 CUPS

Put all the ingredients in a bowl and whisk together.

Can be stored in a glass jar with a tight-fitting lid for up to 1 week.

Use with fish according to the recipe above, or add 1–2 tablespoons to vegetable and fish stews. You could also brush over chicken or lamb and marinate for 8–24 hours in the fridge. Let the meat come to room temperature then cook as preferred.

Spicy grilled salmon collar

Salmon collar is a lesser known cut that was once thrown away or used for bait. This marinade also works well with salmon belly.

4 salmon collars, about
   900 g/2 lb. in total
3 tablespoons sambal oelek
2 tablespoons toasted sesame
   oil, plus extra for tossing
60 ml/¼ cup mirin
1 tablespoon tamari or
   soy sauce, plus extra
   for seasoning
2 tablespoons freshly
   grated ginger

sea salt and cracked
   black pepper
oil, for brushing the grate
450 g/1 lb. shishito peppers
black sesame seeds,
   to garnish (optional)
sweet chilli sauce, to serve
   (optional)

SERVES 4–6

Place the salmon collars in a ceramic baking dish.

In a medium-sized bowl whisk together the sambal oelek, sesame oil, mirin, tamari and ginger and season with salt and pepper. Pour the marinade over the fish. Cover and refrigerate for 30 minutes.

Remove the fish from the fridge and bring to room temperature. Heat the barbecue/grill to medium-high. Brush the grate with oil.

Toss the shishito peppers in a bowl with a splash of sesame oil just to coat. Place on the grill and cook for about 5 minutes, turning once, until they are charred and soft. Remove to a platter, sprinkle with a dash of tamari, and set aside.

Remove the collars from the marinade and place skin-side down on the grill. Cook for 5 minutes, then turn the collars over and lower the heat or move to a cooler part of the grill and continue to cook for another 10 minutes until crispy and just cooked through.

Remove from the grill and place on a platter. Add the shishito peppers, sprinkle with sea salt and sesame seeds and serve with sweet chilli sauce.

Grilled lobsters
WITH FLAVOURED BUTTERS

Lobsters are so easy to throw on the grill and serve up with flavoured butters. Steam the lobsters first, as this makes the meat juicy and tender.

4 cooked lobsters, about
   900 g/2 lb. each, steamed
   or boiled
oil, for brushing the grate
sea salt and freshly ground
   black pepper
good crusty bread, to serve

NORI SEAWEED BUTTER
2 sheets of nori seaweed,
   crumbled
225 g/2 sticks salted butter

WASABI BUTTER
2 tablespoons wasabi powder
225 g/2 sticks salted butter

GARLIC &
CHILLI BUTTER
6 garlic cloves, peeled
1 jalapeño, roughly chopped
225 g/2 sticks salted butter

SERVES 4

To make the seaweed butter, place the nori and butter in the bowl of a food processor and pulse until smooth. Season with salt and pepper and spoon into a small bowl. Clean the food processor bowl.

Repeat the process with the wasabi and butter by placing in the food processor and pulse to combine, then season with salt and pepper and spoon into a small bowl.

Lastly, place the garlic, jalapeño and butter in the food processor. Pulse to combine completely, season with salt and pepper, and spoon into a small bowl.

Heat the barbecue/grill to medium-high. Brush the grate with oil. Crack the claws and brush the lobsters with olive oil, then season with salt and pepper. Using sharp scissors, cut the underneath of the lobster from top to bottom. Place the lobsters on the grill and cook for 5 minutes, then use tongs to turn them over and continue to cook for another 5 minutes or until the flesh is white and has no translucency. Serve with the flavoured butters.

Coconut & lime shrimp skewers

Himalayan salt blocks are so pretty to look at. You can also cook meat, vegetables and fish on them as they work really well on a grill. Afterwards, rinse under cold water.

900 g/2 lb. peeled prawns/
   shrimp, tails on
400-ml/14-fl oz. can of
   unsweetened coconut milk
1 tablespoon curry powder
1 tablespoon ground turmeric
1 tablespoon finely minced
   fresh ginger
1 teaspoon chilli/hot red pepper
   flakes

3 tablespoons fish sauce
35 g/½ cup dried coconut flakes
16 kaffir lime leaves
limes, for squeezing
Himalayan pink salt block
*8 wooden skewers, soaked
   in cold water for 30 minutes*

SERVES 4

Rinse the prawns/shrimp under cold running water and pat dry with paper towels. Place in a ceramic baking dish.

In a medium-sized bowl, whisk together the coconut milk, curry powder, turmeric, ginger, chilli/hot red pepper flakes and fish sauce. Pour the marinade over the prawns/shrimp and add the coconut flakes. Toss to make sure they are completely covered. Cover and refrigerate until ready to use.

Place the salt block on a cold grill/barbecue and heat to 200°C (400°F). Once it has reached this temperature, let the salt block continue to heat for another 30 minutes.

While the block is heating, prepare the skewers. Remove the prawns/shrimp from the refrigerator and divide into eight portions. Thread onto the wooden skewers, alternating with the lime leaves. Brush the prawns/shrimp with a little more of the marinade, then discard any remaining.

Place the skewers on the salt block and cook for 4 minutes, then turn them over and continue to cook for another 4 minutes until the centres of the prawns/shrimp are opaque. Serve with limes for squeezing over.

Garlic chilli shrimp

You can use any type of prawn/shrimp that has the head and shell intact, simply increase the cooking time slightly for larger ones.

900 g/2 lb. prawns/shrimp,
   heads on
1 whole head of garlic
1 tablespoon chilli/hot red
   pepper flakes
60 ml/¼ cup olive oil

2 tablespoons fresh
   oregano leaves
sea salt and cracked
   black pepper
good crusty bread, to serve

SERVES 4–6

Place the prawns/shrimp in a large bowl and set aside.

Break the garlic head into cloves, peel and place in the bowl of a food processor along with the chilli/hot red pepper flakes and olive oil. Process until the garlic is broken into small chunks.

Pour the garlic mixture over the prawns/shrimp and sprinkle with the oregano leaves. Season with salt and pepper and toss to combine. Set aside for 5 minutes.

Heat the barbecue/grill to medium-high.

Place a large cast-iron pan on the grill and heat until just smoking. Place the prawns/shrimp and all the juices in the hot pan and cook for 6–8 minutes, turning every few minutes until they are cooked through. Cook a little longer if the prawns/shrimp are larger. Serve alongside a basket of crusty bread.

Prawn & beef satays

Satays are found all over South-east Asia. They are very easy to make and taste simply wonderful. Perfect for a beach-side cook-up.

20 uncooked prawns/shrimp
250 g/9 oz. fillet steak
dipping sauces, to serve

PRAWN/SHRIMP MARINADE
1 teaspoon coriander seeds
$\frac{1}{2}$ teaspoon cumin seeds
1 garlic clove, crushed
1 teaspoon grated fresh ginger
2 kaffir lime leaves, shredded
1 teaspoon ground turmeric
1 tablespoon light soy sauce
4 tablespoons coconut milk
$\frac{1}{2}$ teaspoon salt

BEEF MARINADE
1 garlic clove, crushed
2 stalks of lemongrass, trimmed
   and finely chopped
1 tablespoon grated fresh ginger
4 coriander/cilantro roots,
   finely chopped
1 red chilli/chile, finely chopped
grated zest and juice of 1 lime
1 tablespoon Thai fish sauce
1 tablespoon dark soy sauce
$1\frac{1}{2}$ tablespoons sugar
1 tablespoon sesame oil
freshly ground black pepper
*40 wooden skewers soaked in
   cold water for 30 minutes*

SERVES 4

Shell and devein the prawns/shrimp, wash them under cold running water and pat dry with kitchen paper/paper towels. Put them into a shallow dish.

To make the prawn/shrimp marinade, put the coriander and cumin seeds into a dry frying pan/skillet and toast over medium heat until golden and aromatic. Remove, let cool slightly, then transfer to a spice grinder (or clean coffee grinder). Add the garlic, ginger and lime leaves and grind to a coarse paste. Alternatively, use a mortar and pestle.

Transfer to a bowl, add the turmeric, soy sauce, coconut milk and salt and mix well. Pour over the prawns/shrimp and let marinate in the refrigerator for 1 hour.

To make the beef satays, cut the fillet steak across the grain into thin strips. Mix all the beef marinade ingredients in a shallow dish, add the beef strips and let marinate for about 1 hour.

Preheat the barbecue/grill. To assemble the beef satays, thread the beef strips onto the skewers, zig-zagging back and forth as you go. To assemble the prawn/shrimp satays, thread the prawns/shrimp lengthways onto the skewers.

Cook both kinds of satays over hot coals for 2 minutes each side, brushing the beef marinade over the beef satays half-way through.

Serve hot with your choice of dipping sauces.

Sriracha & lime grilled chicken wings

You can also use regular lime juice and leaves in this dish to add a pleasant, cooling contrast to all the spices. Chicken wings are fun appetizer to hand around or to take to the beach for a picnic.

24 chicken wings
60 ml/¼ cup Sriracha
60 ml/¼ cup sambal oelek
180 ml/¾ cup dark runny honey, such as avocado
125 ml/½ cup toasted sesame oil
4 garlic cloves
2 kaffir limes, or regular limes, quartered
6 kaffir lime leaves, or regular lime leaves, shredded

1 small onion, roughly chopped
sea salt and cracked black pepper
1 tablespoon black sesame seeds
oil, for brushing the grate
tangerine wedges, to serve

SERVES 4–6

Rinse the chicken wings under running cold water and pat dry with kitchen paper/paper towels. Place in a large ceramic dish or bowl.

Place the Sriracha, sambal oelek, honey, sesame oil, garlic, lime quarters, lime leaves, and onion in a blender and process until you have a smooth sauce. Season with salt and pepper. Pour the sauce over the chicken wings and toss to coat. Cover and refrigerate for 4 hours or overnight.

When you are ready to cook, remove the chicken wings from the fridge and bring to room temperature.

Heat the barbecue/grill to medium-high. Brush the grate with oil.

Cook the wings on the grill for 6–8 minutes, then turn them over and either turn the heat down or move to a cooler part of the grill. Continue to cook for a further 8 minutes, turning occasionally to make sure they are cooked through and crispy on the outside.

Place the cooked wings on a large plate and sprinkle with the sesame seeds. Serve with the tangerine wedges.

Ember-roasted potatoes

Foil-wrapped potatoes baked to perfection with crispy skins and soft, fluffy insides...

4 medium baking potatoes
butter
sea salt and freshly ground black pepper

SERVES 4

Heat a charcoal or wood-fired barbecue/grill.

Wrap the potatoes individually in a double layer of foil and as soon as the coals are glowing red, put the potatoes on top. Rake the charcoal up and around them, but without covering them. Let cook for about 25 minutes, then using tongs, turn the potatoes over carefully and cook for a further 25–30 minutes until cooked through.

Remove from the heat and carefully remove the foil, then cut the potatoes in half. Serve, topped with a spoonful of butter, salt and pepper.

Grilled harissa chicken kabobs

Spicy chicken, hot off the grill and served with lemon wedges and cracked green olives is divine. Serve with ice-cold beers and relax. Store the extra harissa in the fridge and use it to flavour stews, pastas or grilled vegetables and to spoon through rice dishes.

12 chicken thighs, skin on, boneless
60 ml/¼ cup honey
225 g/1 cup scratched green olives
lemon wedges, for squeezing
oil, for brushing the grate

FOR THE HARISSA
2 dried Pasilla chillies/chiles
1 dried Ancho chilli/chile
1 roasted red (bell) pepper

2 fresh red Serrano chillies/chiles, roughly chopped
2 teaspoons ground cumin
2 tablespoons tomato purée/paste
1 teaspoon smoked paprika
4 garlic cloves, peeled and bashed
2 tablespoons olive oil
½ teaspoon kosher salt

SERVES 6–8

To make the harissa, place the dried chillies/chiles in a bowl, cover with boiling water, and soak for 30 minutes. Drain the chillies/chiles, reserving a 60 ml/¼ cup of the soaking liquid.

Place the chillies/chiles, reserved liquid, and the remaining harissa ingredients in a blender and blend until you have a rough paste.

Place the chicken thighs in a large ceramic dish. Mix together 4 tablespoons of the harissa paste with the honey. Pour over the chicken and toss to coat completely. Cover and refrigerate for 6–24 hours. (Pour the remaining harissa into a jar with a tight-fitting lid and refrigerate for up to 6 months.)

Remove the chicken from the fridge and thread onto metal skewers. Bring to room temperature.

Heat the barbecue/grill to medium-high. Brush the grate with oil.

Place the skewers skin-side down on the grill and cook for 8 minutes until golden brown and crispy. Turn the skewers over and turn down the heat or move to a cooler part of the grill. Continue to cook for another 15 minutes. Check for doneness by inserting a sharp knife into the chicken to see that the meat is no longer pink and the juices run clear.

Remove the cooked skewers from the grill, cover and rest for 5 minutes. To serve, pile on a plate and sprinkle with the olives and lemon wedges. (If you wish, the lemon wedges can be briefly charred on the grill.)

1 skirt steak, approx. 900 g/2 lb.
250-g/9-oz. buckwheat soba noodles
oil, for brushing the grate
coriander/cilantro, to serve
sesame seeds, to serve
sea salt and freshly ground black pepper

FOR THE MARINADE
90 ml/⅓ cup vegetable oil
90 ml/⅓ cup soy sauce
90 ml/⅓ cup toasted sesame oil
90 ml/⅓ cup honey
3 tablespoons sherry
3 tablespoons curry powder
2 tablespoons freshly grated ginger
4 garlic cloves

FOR THE PEANUT SAUCE
2 tablespoons dark honey
2 tablespoons toasted sesame oil
½ onion, roughly chopped
3 spring onions/scallions, chopped
2 tablespoons peanut butter
2 tablespoons rice wine vinegar

SERVES 4

Korean steak & noodles

Beautifully charred on the outside and ruby-red rare inside is how this steak comes off the hot coals. Sliced and nestled on top of peanut noodles, it's the perfect food for summer. Serve with Cucumber Pickles (see page 74) and a few green tomatoes.

To make the marinade, place the vegetable oil, soy sauce, sesame oil, honey, sherry, curry powder, ginger and garlic in a blender and process to a smooth sauce. Season with salt and pepper.

Place the steak in a ceramic baking dish. Pour the marinade over the steak, turning the meat to make sure it is completely covered. Cover and refrigerate for 8–24 hours.

When you are ready to cook, remove the steak from the fridge and bring to room temperature.

Cook the soba noodles according to the packet instructions. Rinse under cold water and set aside.

To make the peanut sauce, place the honey, sesame oil, onion, scallions/spring onions, peanut butter and vinegar in a blender and process until smooth. Season.

Place the noodles in a large bowl and spoon over 2–3 tablespoons of the sauce. Toss together, making sure the noodles are well coated in the sauce. Sprinkle with cilantro/coriander and sesame seeds.

Heat the barbecue/grill to medium-high. Brush the grate with oil.

Place the steak on the grill and cook for 5 minutes, then turn the steak over and cook for a further 5 minutes for medium rare. Allow a longer time if you prefer the steak medium to well done.

Remove the steak from the grill, cover, and rest for 10 minutes.

Slice the steak against the grain and serve with the noodles. Serve pickles and kimchi alongside.

SUNSET SUPPERS

Glass noodle, shiitake & vegetable steam-fry

This steam-fry supper is speedy to whip up after a day in the sun. Make the flavour bombs in advance, freeze, and use straight from the icebox when you need fresh, zingy seasoning.

FOR STIR-FRYING
200 g/7 oz. Korean glass noodles (made from sweet potato) or other glass noodles
1 tablespoon sesame oil, plus extra for loosening
300 g/10½ oz. shiitake mushrooms, sliced
300 g/10½ oz. mixed stir-fry vegetables, chopped
3 flavour bomb cubes (see right)
Braggs Liquid Aminos
toasted mixed seeds

FLAVOUR BOMBS
400 g/14 oz. fresh ginger, chopped
3 whole heads of garlic cloves, peeled
3 red chillies/chiles, 2 deseeded
2 bunches spring onions/scallions, trimmed and chopped
1 large bunch coriander/cilantro
1 small bunch of Thai basil
1 bunch of flat-leaf parsley
2 teaspoons turmeric powder
freshly squeezed juice and zest of 3 limes

SERVES 2

To make the flavour bombs, place all the ingredients into a food processor and pulse until a smooth paste is formed, adding splashes of water as needed to loosen it to a smooth paste.

Fill ice-cube trays with paste leaving a little space as they will expand when they freeze. If you do not want to use trays you can freeze blobs in squares of tightly wrapped clingfilm/plastic wrap.

Once frozen, tip all the cubes into a resealable plastic bag so you have them to hand as and when you need them.

Cook the glass noodles in a large pan of boiling water for around 5 minutes; they should still be al dente. Drain and rinse with cold water, return them to the pan and mix with a splash of sesame oil to stop them from sticking together.

When ready to steam-fry, heat the tablespoon of sesame oil in a wok or frying pan/skillet and fry the flavour bomb cubes until fragrant (taking care not to burn them). Add the mushrooms and vegetables and a splash of water from the kettle and steam fry until cooked but al dente.

Add the noodles and season with Braggs Liquid Aminos and some toasted mixed seeds.

Enjoy how virtuous this healthful umami mix makes you feel!

Fried & steamed salmon IN MISO GARLIC SAUCE

This native recipe from Hokkaido, Japan's most northern island, consists of pan-frying (yaki) salmon and some assorted vegetables, then steaming the lot in sake and serving it in miso sauce. Add a little garlic to the miso sauce for an extra burst of flavour.

1 tablespoon vegetable oil
2 skin-on salmon fillets
1/4 Savoy cabbage, diced into bite-sized pieces
1 medium onion, thinly sliced
1/2 carrot, peeled and cut into matchsticks
60 g/2¼ oz. fresh shimeji mushrooms, bottoms trimmed and separated
2 tablespoons sake
1 tablespoon butter, to serve

MISO GARLIC SAUCE
2 garlic cloves, grated
3 tablespoons red miso
2 tablespoons mirin
large frying pan/skillet with a lid

SERVES 2

For the miso garlic sauce, in a small bowl, combine the grated garlic with the red miso and mirin, then stir until combined. Set aside.

Heat the vegetable oil in the large frying pan/skillet over a high heat. Fry both the salmon fillets, skin-side down for 2–3 minutes, or until the skin has browned.

Flip over and fry for 2 more minutes, then remove the salmon from the pan and set aside.

Add all the vegetables and mushrooms to the hot pan and stir-fry for 2 minutes.

Put the salmon fillets back into the pan, nestled among the vegetables, and pour in the sake around the salmon. Place a lid over the frying pan/skillet and let the fish steam over a medium heat for 1 minute to cook off the alcohol.

Add the miso garlic sauce to the pan and stir gently to evenly coat the ingredients. Put the lid back on and simmer for 4–5 minutes over a medium-high heat until the salmon is perfectly cooked all the way through.

When ready to serve, top each salmon fillet with a sliver of butter and allow it to melt a little. Serve hot.

Maple soy salmon

Take care not to overdo the maple syrup as the dish loses something if it is too sweet. This method also works very well with chicken thighs.

60 ml/1/4 cup maple syrup
1 tablespoon soy sauce
1–2 garlic cloves, crushed
pinch of ground ginger or a 2.5-cm/1-inch piece of grated fresh ginger

sea salt and freshly ground black pepper
2 salmon fillets

SERVES 2

In a small bowl, mix together the maple syrup, soy sauce, garlic and ginger and season to taste with salt and pepper.

Place the salmon fillets in an ovenproof dish and coat them on all sides with the mixture.

If time permits, cover with clingfilm/plastic wrap and leave to marinate in the refrigerator for 30–60 minutes.

When ready to cook, preheat the oven to 200°C (400°F) Gas 6. Cook the salmon in the ovenproof dish, uncovered, for around 15–30 minutes, until its centre is cooked through.

Sunshine laksa WITH CRAB & SNOW PEAS

This recipe is so bright, so sunny and yet tastes so delicate! It is a great illustration of subtle umami flavours. You can replace the millet with brown rice, quinoa or any healthy grain of your choice.

200 g/1 cup millet
1 tablespoon vegetable oil
2 x 400-ml/14-oz. cans coconut milk
500 ml/2 cups chicken stock
500 ml/2 cups water
2 tablespoons fish sauce
5 kaffir lime leaves
1 lemongrass stalk, crushed
freshly squeezed juice of 3 limes
250 g/9 oz. white crab meat
200 g/3 small handfuls mangetout/snow peas, cut on the diagonal into 1-cm/½-inch pieces
4 spring onions/scallions, finely chopped

TO SERVE
2 red chillies/chiles, deseeded and finely chopped
1 handful of coriander/cilantro, chopped
lime wedges

LAKSA PASTE
3 shallots, cut in half
3 garlic cloves
3 red chillies/chiles, (try 1 with the seeds left in and 2 deseeded; leave more with seeds in if you want it hotter)
2 lemongrass stalks, chopped
2.5-cm/1-inch square piece of ginger, roughly chopped
1½ tablespoons any nut or seed butter
2 teaspoons shrimp paste
2 teaspoons curry powder
½ teaspoon salt
1 tablespoon vegetable oil

SERVES 4

Place all the laksa paste ingredients in a small food processor and blitz to a paste.

Cook the millet according to the packet instructions, set aside and leave covered.

Heat the oil in a large heavy-based saucepan over a high heat. Add the laksa paste and cook for 1 minute to release all the aromatics.

Add the coconut milk, chicken stock, water, fish sauce, kaffir lime leaves and lemongrass to the pot and bring to the boil for 10 minutes. Remove from the heat and add the lime juice.

Take some warm serving bowls and in the base put ½ tablespoons of millet, ½ tablespoons crab meat, one-quarter of the mangetout/snow peas and some spring onions/scallions and ladle over the piping hot broth.

Serve with the red chillies/chiles, coriander/cilantro and lime wedges.

Lobster quesadillas

Lobster is a luxurious ingredient that requires a bit of an event to justify it, but it's well worth it and these quesadillas will take centre stage when having a summer cook-up with your friends.

1 medium lobster tail or 8 langoustines
a knob/pat of butter
a little vegetable oil
freshly squeezed juice of 1 lime
8 corn tortillas
200 g/2 cups grated Cheddar cheese, or similar
1 ripe avocado, peeled, stoned and thinly sliced
salsa or Tabasco sauce, to drizzle
handful of coriander/cilantro leaves, to garnish

FOR THE
CARAMELIZED ONIONS
1 red onion
a knob/pat of butter
1 tablespoon demerara/turbinado sugar

SERVES 4

First make the caramelized onions. Slice the onion into very thin rings. Melt the knob/pat of butter in a pan, add the onion rings and slowly sauté until soft. Add the sugar and continue cooking with the lid on for approx. 15 minutes until they have a jammy consistency; if dry, add a little water.

To prepare the lobster or langoustines, use scissors to cut down the shell, making sure you don't snag the meat when you do this. Heat the knob/pat of butter and a little oil in a frying pan/skillet, add the lobster or langoustines and sauté over a medium-high heat for 3 minutes on each side until just barely cooked through (it/they will finish cooking in the heated quesadillas). Add the lime juice to deglaze the pan and set aside to cool.

Remove the lobster meat from the shell and chop into bite-sized pieces.

Place a corn tortilla in a cast iron frying pan/skillet preheated to a medium-high temperature. Quickly place a handful of Cheddar on top and spread out. Scatter a quarter of the lobster or langoustine meat over, add a tablespoon of the caramelized onions, add a little more cheese, then top with another corn tortilla.

When the bottom tortilla is warmed through, you will be able to lift a corner and see some charring, then flip it over to the other side using a spatula and heat to the same slightly charred level. Beware of overcooking – they should be slightly charred. Repeat with the remaining tortillas and filling.

Tip the cooled lobster cooking juices over the sliced avocado and serve on the side with a drizzle of salsa to taste and scattered with coriander/cilantro leaves.

Hand-dived scallops

WITH VANILLA RISOTTO & PEA SHOOTS

Surprisingly vanilla goes really well with fish and seafood as demonstrated in this scallop risotto. If you're looking for a recipe to impress your friends, try this one.

1 litre/quart chicken stock

2 vanilla pods/beans

4 hand-dived scallops in shell, shirked and cleaned (reserve corals – the curved orange part – for the sauce)

a knob/pat of butter

1 tablespoon olive oil

1 small white onion, diced

200 g/1 cup carnaroli rice

250 ml/1 cup white wine

50 g/²⁄₃ cup grated Parmesan

120 ml/¹⁄₂ cup white port

560 ml/1 pint fish stock

560 ml/1 pint single/light cream

1 bay leaf

1 star anise

1 teaspoon vanilla paste, or 1 vanilla pod/bean, (seeds only)

sunflower or unrefined sesame oil

sea salt and freshly ground black pepper

olive oil

a handful of pea shoots

SERVES 4

Simmer the chicken stock gently and add two split vanilla pods/beans. Remove from the heat and allow to infuse (overnight is best, but a few hours is fine).

Prepare the scallops and remove all of the skirt and trim. Dry them on kitchen paper/paper towels.

To make the risotto, add a knob/pat of butter and a generous splash of olive oil to a frying pan/skillet. Soften, but do not colour, the onions for around 5 minutes. Add the rice and constantly stir until it turns shiny, about 2 minutes. Slowly add the white wine and then the set-aside chicken stock over a 20–30 minute period, stirring repeatedly until the risotto is fully cooked. Add the Parmesan.

For the sauce, reduce the port, fish stock and cream in a saucepan with the bay leaf, star anise and vanilla paste or seeds. Bring to the boil, then reduce to a simmer and add the scallop corals. Cook for a further 5 minutes. Blitz the sauce with a stick blender and pass through a fine sieve/strainer into a pan. Re-aerate the sauce with the blender just before serving.

Oil the scallops with sunflower or unrefined sesame oil and season. To cook the scallops, get a non-stick frying pan/skillet really hot, until it is smoking. Place them into the pan/skillet presentation-side down (that's the slightly larger of the two sides). Allow to cook for about 90 seconds (times vary depending on scallop size) take off the heat, turn the scallops and cook each for a further 90 seconds. Season lightly with some crushed sea salt.

To plate up, place the risotto on the middle of the plate, pop the scallop on top, and fill the base of the serving bowl with the light, aerated sauce. Drizzle a little olive oil around the plate and garnish with the pea shoots on the side.

Serve with a chilled Sauvignon Blanc or a nice glass of Billecart-Salmon Champagne for indulgent, decadent dining.

Garlic, chili & parsley prawns

The Mediterranean flavours along with a hint of oriental fish sauce combine to create a taste sensation. This is also amazing on pasta.

1 whole head of garlic, thinly sliced
1 fresh red chilli/chile (with seeds), finely chopped
4 tablespoons olive oil, plus a splash
500 g/1 lb. 2 oz. fresh prawns/shrimp, heads, tails and shells on
1 tablespoon fish sauce, plus an extra splash
100 ml/7 tablespoons dry white wine
freshly ground black pepper
50 g/3 tablespoons butter, at room temperature
1 teaspoon tomato purée/paste
1 large handful flat-leaf parsley, finely chopped

SERVES 2

Heat half the garlic and chilli/chile in a large frying pan/skillet with some olive oil.

Add the whole prawns/shrimp with 1 tablespoon fish sauce, half the white wine, and lots of freshly ground black pepper. Stir frequently and allow the prawns/shrimp to cook. They will go from grey to pink in about 2–3 minutes.

Remove the prawns/shrimp from the pan/skillet and take the pan off the heat. Remove the heads and shells to leave you with just the juicy, pink flesh.

Put the pan/skillet back onto a high heat, with a small splash of oil and the rest of the garlic and chilli. When the garlic begins to colour, deglaze the pan/skillet with the remaining white wine and, when this begins to evaporate, toss the peeled prawns/shrimp back into the pan with the butter, a small splash of fish sauce and the tomato purée/paste. Shake and toss well until this glossy sauce coats all the prawns/shrimp. Take the pan/skillet off the heat and toss through lots of fresh parsley. Serve immediately.

Monkfish with mango & avocado salsa

You can replace the monkfish with any sustainable meaty white fish fillet and substitute the mango for ripe strawberries (change the herbs to basil and parsley if you do, though).

350–400 g/12½–14 oz. monkfish tail, trimmed
sea salt and freshly ground black pepper
squeeze of lemon juice
drizzle of olive oil

MANGO SALSA
8 tablespoons extra virgin olive oil
good squeeze of lemon juice, to taste
1 tablespoon Worcestershire sauce
splash of balsamic vinegar
2 handfuls chopped coriander/cilantro
1 handful chopped mint
1 large ripe but firm mango, peeled, stoned/pitted and cubed
1 large avocado, peeled, stoned/pitted and cubed

SERVES 2

Preheat the oven to 180°C (350°F) Gas 4. Line an ovenproof dish with baking parchment.

Cut the monkfish into 4 medallions, each about 1.5-cm/¾-inch thick (ask the fishmonger to do this for you). Place the monkfish in the dish, season with salt and pepper and add a squeeze of lemon juice. Drizzle with olive oil and bake for 15 minutes or until the fish is cooked through.

While the fish is cooking, prepare the salsa: mix the oil, lemon juice, Worcestershire sauce, balsamic vinegar and herbs. Season with salt and pepper, then stir in the mango and avocado cubes.

Place 2 monkfish medallions on each plate, spoon over salsa and plenty of the dressing from the bottom of the bowl.

Sake mussels

A stunning recipe for mussels, this tastes unlike any other mussel recipe. Serve with plenty of chopped fresh herbs, more sake and some crusty bread to mop up the juices.

1 kg/2 lb. 3 oz. cultivated mussels, rinsed and scrubbed
250 ml/1 cup sake
2 tablespoons umami paste (available from larger stores)
4 teaspoons finely chopped garlic
4 teaspoons finely chopped fresh ginger
2 large, ripe tomatoes, chopped
fresh flat-leaf parsley and chives, chopped, to serve

SERVES 2

Make sure the mussels are clean and any tendrils ('beards') are removed from the sides of the shells. Discard any that are open or open when tapped.

Mix the sake with the umami paste, garlic, and ginger in a small bowl.

Place a large saucepan with a tight-fitting lid over a high heat.

When hot, add the mussels, sake mixture and tomatoes and cover tightly with the lid. Steam for 3–4 minutes.

When the mussels are cooked, the shells should have opened. Discard any mussels that are still closed.

Place the mussels and sauce in a serving bowl and scatter with parsley and chives.

Spicy tuna & black rice bowl

This recipe deconstructs sushi tuna rolls to make a sophisticated and healthful meal in a bowl. If you like it really spicy, add a pinch of Shichimi Togarashi (Japanese 7 Spice Powder).

240 g/1 cup plus 3 tablespoons black rice
60 g/4 tablespoons wild rice
1 tablespoon sesame oil
560 g/1¼ lbs. fresh, sushi-grade tuna, chopped into 1-cm/¼-inch cubes
¼ cucumber, deseeded and chopped into 1-cm/¼-inch cubes
1 ripe but firm avocado, chopped into 1-cm/¼-inch cubes
6 spring onions/scallions, finely sliced
2.5-cm/1-inch piece fresh ginger, finely grated
2 tablespoons soy sauce
4 sheets nori
furikake seasoning or toasted sesame seeds
2–4 limes, to serve

SPICY MAYONNAISE
4 tablespoons mayonnaise (preferably Japanese mayonnaise if you can find it)
¼ teaspoon tomato ketchup
Sriracha hot sauce or Tabasco, to taste

SERVES 4

Cook the rices together in a large pot of boiling salted water until tender but still al dente with a nice bite but not raw. This should take about 35 minutes. Drain well. Place in a bowl and mix in the sesame oil while the rice is still hot. Set aside to cool.

To make the tuna mixture, combine the tuna, cucumber, avocado, spring onions/scallions, ginger and soy sauce.

Make the spicy mayonnaise sauce by mixing the mayonnaise and ketchup with as much Sriracha or Tabasco sauce as you can handle.

Prepare the nori garnish by folding each sheet of nori over four times, and then slicing it into thin shreds.

Assemble the dish. For each person, spoon about 2–3 tablespoons of rice into a flat bowl. Top with a generous spoonful of the tuna mixture, then gently top with a small spoonful of spicy mayonnaise. Generously scatter nori shreds and a sprinkle of furikake seasoning (or toasted sesame seeds). Serve with half a lime per person.

Thai steamed snapper

WITH STICKY COCONUT JASMINE RICE

Brilliant for a casually sophisticated dinner party, you can also use this versatile marinade for fish fillets. You will win over your guests with the sweet rice and super-savoury but super-light fish. Serve with a crisp green salad.

1 whole red snapper, sea bass or other sustainable white fish, about 2 kg/4½ lbs., descaled, gutted and cleaned

4 limes (1 sliced)

1 bunch fresh coriander/cilantro

1 bunch of spring onions/scallions, topped and sliced (reserve tops for stuffing fish)

1 sweet potato, diced into thumbnail-sized pieces

2.5-cm/1-inch piece of fresh ginger, sliced

5 garlic cloves, peeled

3 lemongrass stalks, outer skin removed and roughly chopped

2 red chillies/chiles, deseeded (keep the seeds of half a chilli/chile only)

3 tablespoons toasted sesame oil

4 tablespoons fish sauce

3 tablespoons soy sauce

1 tablespoon brown sugar or palm sugar

STICKY COCONUT
JASMINE RICE

200 g/1 cup plus 2 tablespoons sticky rice

400-ml/14-oz. can coconut milk

½ teaspoon salt

1 teaspoon caster/granulated sugar

½ teaspoon jasmine green tea (optional)

50 g/⅔ cup desiccated/dried shredded coconut

SERVES 4

Preheat the oven to 200°C (400°F) Gas 6.

Cut a piece of wide baking parchment twice the length of your fish. Fold the parchment in half and then open it, placing one half on a baking sheet. Put the fish on the diagonal on the piece of parchment on the baking sheet.

Make slashes in the fish on the diagonal through the skin down to the bone on both sides. Stuff the cavity with a few slices of lime, half the coriander/cilantro and the tops of the spring onions/scallions. Scatter sweet potato cubes and spring onion/scallion chunks around the fish.

In a food processor, combine the rest of the coriander/cilantro, ginger, garlic, lemongrass and chilli/chile and blitz into a paste.

Add the sesame oil, fish sauce, soy sauce, sugar and the juice of the remaining 3 limes and blitz again.

Rub this marinade all over the fish and fold the other half of parchment over the fish and wrap the edges over to close tightly.

Cook in the preheated oven for 25–30 minutes or until the fish is cooked. To test if the fish is cooked, remove from the oven and take a peek inside a corner of the parcel, but be careful because the steam will escape. If the eye of the fish has turned white, your fish is cooked.

While the fish is in the oven, make the rice. Put the rice in a non-stick medium saucepan (that has a lid), and add the coconut milk, salt, sugar and jasmine tea (if using). Place over a medium heat and bring to the boil. Once boiling, put the lid on the pan and turn the heat down to low. Leave to cook for 15–20 minutes on a really low heat – do not be tempted stir or to lift the lid off before 15 minutes as this will let the steam escape. Turn the heat off and leave the rice until ready to serve. Once the fish is cooked, open the parcel and serve large chunks of fish on the creamy, sticky rice topped with a large spoonful of the cooking juices.

NECTARINE AGRODOLCE

*Agrodolce is an Italian sweet-and-sour sauce.
The basic combination is made up of vinegar and
sugar. This can be achieved in many ways with
different vinegars, honey, syrups, fruit and onions.*

3 tablespoons olive oil
1 white onion, finely diced
235 ml/1 cup white wine vinegar
85 g/¼ cup maple syrup
35 g/¼ cup (golden) raisins
225 g/½ lb. (about 2) ripe
    nectarines, finely diced

sea salt and cracked
    black pepper
*sterilized glass jars with
    airtight lids*

MAKES 475 ML/2 CUPS

Preheat a cast-iron pan over medium heat and pour
in the oil. Swirl the pan to coat. Add the onion and
cook for 6–8 minutes, stirring occasionally, until
golden and tender.

   Add the vinegar, maple syrup and raisins, and
simmer for 10–12 minutes, until the mixture is syrupy.
Add the nectarine and cook for another 5 minutes.
Season with salt and pepper.

   Remove from the heat and set aside to cool at
room temperature. Serve or store in a sterilized
glass jar in the refrigerator for up to 4 days.

Summer chicken

WITH NECTARINE AGRODOLCE

Grilled chicken, marinated in za'atar spices, then cooked over hot coals, is a great treat. The sweet-and-sour taste of the Nectarine Agrodolce adds a delicious tart and sweet flavour to this dish.

1 whole chicken, cut into
   10 pieces
2 tablespoons wholegrain
   mustard
2 tablespoons za'atar spice blend
2 tablespoons clear honey
60 ml/¼ cup olive oil
60 ml/¼ cup red wine vinegar

1 teaspoon sea salt
cracked black pepper,
   for sprinkling
sesame seeds, to serve
   (optional)
Nectarine Agrodolce
   (see left), to serve

SERVES 6

Place the chicken pieces in a ceramic dish. In a small bowl whisk together the wholegrain mustard, za'atar spice blend, honey, oil, vinegar and salt. Pour over the chicken and toss to make sure all the pieces are coated. Sprinkle with pepper, cover and refrigerate for 6–24 hours.

Once marinated, remove the chicken from the refrigerator and bring to room temperature.

Place a grill pan over medium-high heat. Add the chicken skin-side down (or skin-side up if using a broiler/grill) and cook for 8 minutes. Turn the chicken, reduce the heat, and cook for a further 8–10 minutes, turning occasionally. Remove the chicken from the heat, cover, and set aside to rest for 10 minutes.

Sprinkle the grilled chicken pieces with sesame seeds and serve with hot or cold Nectarine Agrodolce.

Chicken Teriyaki WITH LIME ON QUINOA RICE

Supermarkets and grocery stores sell ready-made bottles of the sweet, soy-based teriyaki that you can use to marinate your chicken, salmon or whatever takes your fancy. But nothing beats the taste of a homemade teriyaki sauce. It is very easy to make and after trying this recipe, you might never purchase ready-made teriyaki sauce again!

1 tablespoon vegetable oil

2 leeks, chopped into 2-cm/³⁄₄-inch lengths

500 g/1 lb. 2 oz. boneless skin-on chicken thigh fillets, diced into bite-sized pieces

4 tablespoons katakuriko (potato starch) or cornflour/cornstarch

TERIYAKI SAUCE WITH LIME

3 tablespoons soy sauce

3 tablespoons mirin

1 tablespoon soft light brown sugar

1 tablespoon sake

1 tablespoon lime juice and grated zest from ¹⁄₂ lime

TO SERVE

800 g/6 cups cooked Japanese rice and quinoa, to serve

toasted white and black sesame seeds

yuzu kosho chilli/chili paste, to serve (optional)

SERVES 4

In a small bowl, mix together the soy sauce, mirin, brown sugar, sake, lime juice and zest to make the teriyaki sauce, stirring until the sugar has dissolved. Set aside.

Add ¹⁄₂ tablespoon of the vegetable oil to a frying pan/skillet over a medium heat. Add the leeks and fry until lightly browned on each side. Remove them from the pan and set aside.

Place the chicken pieces in a bowl and lightly toss with the katakuriko (potato starch) or cornflour/cornstarch to evenly coat all over.

Add the remaining ¹⁄₂ tablespoon vegetable oil to the same frying pan/skillet and fry the chicken, skin-side down, for 2 minutes until browned. Remove the pan from the heat briefly and remove the excess chicken fat by tilting the pan to the side and carefully soaking up the fat with 1–2 kitchen paper/paper towels (taking care not to touch the surface of the hot pan with your hand).

Turn the chicken pieces over and cook for 2 minutes on the other side. Add the leeks back into the pan, then pour over the teriyaki sauce, stirring to coat the chicken and leeks evenly. Simmer for 4–5 minutes over a medium-high heat until the sauce has thickened.

Divide the cooked rice and quinoa between serving bowls, then add the teriyaki chicken. Sprinkle with toasted sesame seeds and serve with yuzu kosho chilli/chili paste, if you want some extra heat.

Grilled lamb koftas

Once you master crafting koftas, the permutations are endless. Traditionally made with lamb, you can literally use any minced/ground meat of your choice and experiment with seasoning. Serve these with hot sauce, a good Tzatziki, toasted flat breads or rice and a fresh-tasting chopped salad (little gem hearts, cucumber, red onion and of fresh mint) dressed with olive oil and lemon.

1 onion

1 green (bell) pepper, deseeded

1 extra large handful of flat-leaf parsley

1 extra large handful of mint, leaves only

2 teaspoons tomato purée/paste

1½ teaspoons ground cumin

1½ teaspoons paprika

1 teaspoon ground cinnamon

1 teaspoon ground allspice

fresh nutmeg

sea salt and freshly ground black pepper

400 g/14 oz. finely minced/ground lamb, pork or turkey

50 g/½ cup minus 1 tablespoon toasted pine nuts, chopped

25 g/2 tablespoons raisins

1 egg yolk

250 g/1½ cups cherry tomatoes

2 red onions, cut into skewerable wedges

2 yellow (bell) peppers cut into squares for skewering

6 rashers/slices smoked bacon, cut into 2.5-cm/1-inch squares

olive oil, for cooking

8–10 long wooden skewers, soaked in water for 30 minutes

SERVES 4

Pulse the onion and pepper in a food processor until finely chopped. Remove from processor and squeeze out any liquid through a sieve/strainer. Chop the fresh herbs and place in a large bowl, add the onions, green pepper, tomato purée/paste and spices.

Mix thoroughly and season well with a good grating of nutmeg, salt and plenty of freshly ground black pepper.

Add the minced/ground meat, pine nuts, raisins and egg yolk to the paste and mix well. Shape into kofta balls using lightly oiled hands.

Thread the cherry tomatoes, onion, (bell) peppers and bacon on to the prepared skewers, making sure there is a square of bacon on either side of the kofta ball to keep it moist. Drizzle the koftas with a little olive oil and grill, bake or barbecue, until cooked through and nicely browned.

Simmered beef & tomatoes on rice

Known as Gyu don, this is one of the top five most popular donburi dishes in Japan. It is basically a bowl of rice topped with seasoned, very thinly sliced beef and onion. It's simple to make and hits the spot magically when hunger strikes. Here, some tomatoes have been added to the traditional recipe for extra flavour and a touch of colour.

250 g/9 oz. sirloin steak
50 ml/½ tablespoon sake
2½ tablespoons soy sauce
2 tablespoons mirin
1 tablespoon soft light brown sugar
½ large onion, cut into
   1-cm/½-inch wedges
5 g/⅛ oz. fresh ginger, peeled
   and cut into thin strips
1 large tomato, cut into quarters

TO SERVE
400 g/3 cups cooked white
   Japanese rice
shichimi (Japanese spice mix)

SERVES 2

Slice the sirloin steak as thinly as possible (see tip below) and set aside.

Combine the sake, soy sauce, mirin and brown sugar with 100 ml/⅓ cup plus 1 tablespoon water in a medium saucepan and bring to the boil.

Add the thinly sliced beef, the onion and ginger to the pan and bring to the boil again. Skim off any scum that comes off the surface of the beef. Reduce the heat to low-medium and simmer for 5 minutes, uncovered.

Add the tomato and simmer for another 10 minutes, carefully peeling away then discarding the tomato skins as they soften and start to separate.

Portion some cooked rice into serving bowls, then top with the beef and tomato mixture. Add all the cooking juices so that the rice can absorb the flavours. Sprinkle with shichimi and enjoy.

Tip The easiest way to thinly slice a large piece of meat is to wrap it in clingfilm/plastic wrap and freeze for about 2 hours for a thickness of about 10 cm/4 inches, or a shorter time if the cut is thinner. You want the meat partially frozen, so the outside is firm and the inside is still soft. The texture should almost be the consistency of cured meat, rather than still frozen. This firmness allows it to be sliced much more finely. Unwrap the meat and thinly slice across the grain with a sharp carving knife for the most tender bite. Leave the partially frozen meat at room temperature for 30 minutes to thaw out a little before using, or place back in the freezer for when next needed.

DESSERTS & DRINKS

Thai fruit salad

You can put any combination of tropical fruits together into a colourful and juicy salad that will sparkle like a bowl of gems. If you can't find roseapples, you may like to add a teaspoonful of rosewater to the lemon juice mixture.

1 small ripe papaya
½ pineapple
1 ripe mango
4 Asian rose-apples (optional)
   or small, regular apples
1 ripe guava

1 tablespoon freshly squeezed
lemon or lime juice
1 tablespoon sugar
10 mint leaves, finely chopped,
   to serve

SERVES 4

Peel, halve and deseed the papaya. Cut the flesh into small cubes.

Peel, core, and cube the pineapple.

Cut the cheeks off the mango, cut the flesh in diamond shapes down to the skin, turn the cheeks inside out, then scoop off the pieces with a fork.

To prepare the rose apples, cut them in half, cut out the cores and cut the flesh into small cubes.

Cut the guava in half, scoop out and discard the seeds, then cut the flesh into small cubes.

Arrange the fruit in a bowl. Add the lemon juice, sugar and chopped mint. Mix well and chill in the refrigerator before serving.

Lychee sorbet

While many fruits are suitable for making mouth-watering and cleansing sorbets, perhaps the most cooling is lychee sorbet. If you cannot find fresh lychees in your neighbourhood, this recipe is also good with canned lychees.

150 g/1 cup plus 2 tablespoons
   sugar
500 g/18 oz. fresh lychees,
   peeled, deseeded and finely
   chopped, or about 450 g/
   16 oz. canned lychees,

drained and chopped
a few fresh lychees, to serve
   (optional)
an electric ice cream maker
   (optional)

SERVES 4

To make a sugar syrup, put the sugar in a saucepan with 300 ml/1¼ cups water. Bring to the boil and stir until the sugar dissolves. Let cool.

Put the lychees in a blender, add the cooled syrup and blend until smooth. Freeze for about 1 hour until the mixture is slushy and frozen around the edges. Remove from the freezer, transfer to the blender,

blend again, then return the mixture to the freezer for about 30 minutes. Alternatively, if you have an electric ice cream maker, churn until the mixture is completely frozen. Transfer to a freezer-proof container and freeze until ready to serve.

Before serving, let soften in the refrigerator for about 20 minutes, then serve in scoops with a few fresh lychees, if available.

Notes This recipe is suitable for many fruits. In particular, try papaya, pineapple, kiwifruit and mango.

Make extra sugar syrup, then decant into a storage bottle and keep in the refrigerator for use in drinks and desserts. It is a very useful ingredient.

Coconut ice cream

*Everywhere in Thailand, the most common
flavouring used in ice cream manufacture
is coconut. It offers a rich, fresh-yet-creamy
taste and is lighter than dairy ice cream.
Top with toasted coconut or even raw cocoa
nibs for a deliciously tropical treat.*

600 ml/2½ cups coconut milk
300 ml/1 whipping cream
150 g/⅔ cup sugar
2 eggs
3 tablespoons desiccated
    coconut, lightly toasted in

a dry frying pan/skillet
a small loaf pan or similar
a freezer-proof container
an electric ice cream maker
    (optional)

SERVES 4

Put the coconut milk, whipping cream and sugar in
saucepan and bring to the boil. Remove from the heat.

Put the eggs in a bowl and whisk well. Gradually
whisk the boiled coconut milk mixture into the eggs,
then let cool completely and chill.

When cold, pour the mixture into a small loaf pan,
cover and freeze until firm. Chop up the ice cream,
then beat until smooth, using an electric mixer or
food processor. Spoon the mixture back into the loaf
pan, cover and freeze for several hours until firm.

Alternatively, if you have an electric ice cream
maker, churn until the mixture is completely frozen.
Transfer to a freezer-proof container and freeze until
ready to serve.

Serve sprinkled with the toasted coconut.

Coconut frozen yogurt WITH STRAWBERRIES

Fresh and light with only a fraction of the fat of ice cream, frozen yogurt is the natural choice for the health conscious. All you need is a freezer!

700 ml/1 lb. 8 oz. plain
   soy yogurt
340 ml/1½ cups coconut milk
100 ml/⅓ cup plus 1 tablespoon
   agave syrup
2 teaspoons lemon juice

desiccated coconut, to serve
strawberries, to serve
*an electric ice cream maker
   (optional)*

SERVES 6–8

Put the yogurt, milk, agave syrup and lemon juice in a bowl and mix until smooth. If you have an ice cream maker, use this to churn the mixture according to the manufacturer's instructions.

If you don't have an ice cream maker, pour the mixture into a freezerproof container (wide, flat, metal trays work well as the mixture freezes more quickly) and freeze. After 30 minutes, or when the edges are beginning to freeze, remove the container from the freezer and whisk thoroughly to break down the ice crystals. Return to the freezer and repeat this process intermittently until completely frozen, but do not let it go rock hard, as you want to be able to scoop it out easily. If you want it super smooth, you can blitz it in a food processor when it is just frozen. Scoop into a bowl and serve with strawberries and desiccated coconut over the top.

The variations for this are endless. For a plain version, use rice milk instead of coconut milk. Add any blitzed up fruit or cocoa powder. Play around with it!

Mojito sorbet

The ubiquitous mojito cocktail, made into a tangy sorbet. You also have the added value of being able to use any leftover sorbet to make a killer mojito smoothie!

170 g/1 cup xylitol
5 sprigs of fresh mint plus
   2 tablespoons freshly
   chopped leaves

grated zest and juice of 2 limes
an ice cream maker (optional)

SERVES 6–8

Put 500 ml/2 cups water, the xylitol and mint sprigs in a saucepan and bring to the boil. Reduce the heat to a minimum and simmer for 5 minutes.

Remove from the heat and strain the liquid, squeezing as much liquid as possible out of the sprigs. Immediately, while the liquid is still hot, add the lime zest. Allow the mixture to cool slightly, then add the lime juice and chopped mint leaves. Refrigerate to cool thoroughly.

If you have an ice cream maker, use this to churn the mixture according to the manufacturer's instructions. If you don't have an ice cream maker, pour the mixture into a freezerproof container (wide, flat, metal trays work well as the mixture freezes more quickly) and freeze. After 20 minutes, or when the edges are beginning to freeze, remove the container from the freezer and whisk thoroughly to break down the ice crystals. This will ensure a smooth sorbet. Return to the freezer and repeat this process intermittently until the sorbet is frozen.

Tutti fruitti semifreddo WITH CANDIED CITRUS

The really great thing about making a semifreddo is that you don't need an ice cream maker. It freezes wonderfully in a container and you can serve it either in scoops or turned out onto serving plate and sliced.

3 UK medium/US large eggs
2 egg yolks
100 g/½ cup caster/granulated sugar
500 ml/2 cups double/heavy cream

3 tablespoons Candied Citrus (see below), finely chopped
cookies, to serve
an electric hand whisk

SERVES 6–8

Combine the eggs, yolks and sugar in a heatproof bowl and place over a pot of simmering water. Whisk the mixture with an electric hand whisk on a high speed for about 5 minutes, until it turns into pale yellow ribbons and has thickened. Turn off the heat and place the bowl with the egg mixture over a bowl filled with iced water to cool.

Pour the cream into a large bowl and beat until thick, and soft peaks form. Fold the cooled egg mixture through the cream until thoroughly incorporated. Fold in the candied fruit and pour into a clean bowl. Cover and freeze until firm.

Scoop and serve with cookies.

Note You can also line a loaf pan with clingfilm/plastic wrap and pour in the semifreddo. Once frozen invert the pan onto a serving plate and unmould. Cut into 4-cm/1½-inch slices to serve.

CANDIED CITRUS

This may seem a little laborious but it reaps huge rewards and you will never look at candied citrus in the same way again. You can juice the oranges once peeled and refrigerate for later.

6 lemons or 4 oranges or 8 limes
700 g/3½ cups superfine/caster sugar
a baking sheet, sprinkled with superfine/caster sugar

MAKES 475 ML/2 CUPS

Peel the oranges into strips making sure you get no pith on the peel. Cut the peels into thin matchsticks and set aside.

Bring a small pan of water to the boil and drop the peel into it. Cook for 10 minutes. Drain the peel and repeat the process. This will get rid of any bitterness in the peel.

Bring the sugar and 700 ml/3 cups of water to a boil over a medium-high heat. Reduce the heat and simmer for 5 minutes, stirring occasionally, until the sugar has completely dissolved. Add the peel and bring to a boil, then reduce the heat to a rapid simmer. Continue to cook for another 20 minutes brushing down the sides with a pastry brush as necessary. Turn off the heat and allow the citrus to cool in the syrup for at least 1 hour.

Preheat the oven to 120°C (250°F) Gas ½.

Remove the peel from the pan with a slotted spoon, shaking any excess syrup back into the pan. Toss the peel in the sugar on the prepared baking sheet and bake in the preheated oven for 45 minutes. Remove from the oven and allow to cool before serving. Store in airtight containers for up to 6 months.

Matcha ice cream WITH BLACK SESAME PRALINE

Delicious green tea ice cream with sweet crunchy sesame praline is a feast for the eyes! Matcha dissolves quickly in either hot or cold water to make a refreshing drink.

500 ml/2 cups whole milk
2 tablespoons powdered matcha green tea
250 ml/1 cup double/heavy cream
150 g/3/4 cup cane sugar
6 egg yolks

FOR THE PRALINE
1 tablespoon toasted sesame oil
300 g/1½ cups cane sugar
70 g/½ cup black sesame seeds

SERVES 6–8

In a small bowl whisk together 80 ml/1/3 cup of the milk and the matcha powder and let sit for 5 minutes.

Pour the remaining milk into a saucepan, whisk in the cream and matcha mix, and then cook over a medium heat until just below boiling point.

In a medium-sized bowl whisk together the sugar and egg yolks. Slowly pour in the hot milk, whisking continuously, then pour back into the saucepan. Stir over a low heat until the mixture is thick and coats the back of wooden spoon. Set aside to cool to room temperature, then place in the fridge for 4 hours.

Freeze the chilled custard in an ice cream maker according to the manufacturer's instructions. Store in an airtight container in the freezer until ready to use.

To make the praline, brush a baking sheet with the sesame oil and set aside. Place the sugar in a saucepan with 80 ml/1/3 cup water over a high heat and cook for 6–8 minutes until dark golden brown. Do not stir.

Pour evenly over the prepared baking sheet and sprinkle with the sesame seeds. Set aside to harden. Break into chunks and serve with scoops of the ice cream.

Spicy dark chocolate & coconut pots

These dark little chocolate pots are a dream to eat and a dream to make. This is a simple recipe that can be whisked up quickly and ahead of time. Ancho chilli/chili powder adds a little kick, but you can use any kind of spice to give it an extra flavour dimension.

340 g/12 oz. extra dark/ bittersweet chocolate, 70% cocoa solids, finely chopped
2 teaspoons ground Ancho chilli/chili powder
½ teaspoon ground cinnamon

2 x 400-ml/14-oz. cans of coconut milk
chocolate, to decorate (chilled)

SERVES 6

Break up the chocolate and place in a large bowl. Add the chilli/chili powder and cinnamon.

In a medium-sized saucepan bring the coconut milk to the boil over a medium-high heat. Pour the hot milk over the chocolate and stir until it has completely melted.

Pour the chocolate mixture into six small bowls or ramekins. Cover and place in the fridge for about 1½ hours until set.

When ready to serve, remove from the fridge and grate a little chocolate over each pot – it's easier to do this if the chocolate has been chilled first.

Yogurt panna cotta WITH FIG SPOON FRUIT

This dessert is so simple and delicate. Adorned with plump fig spoon fruits, it is a feast for the eyes. It works really well as a dessert for a weekend get-together.

2 teaspoons gelatin powder
235 ml/1 cup double/heavy
    cream
355 ml/1½ cups whole milk
50 g/¼ cup superfine/caster
    sugar
1 vanilla pod/bean, halved and
    seeds removed

430 g/2 cups natural set yogurt
2 teaspoons grated lemon zest
Fig Spoon Fruit (see below),
    to serve
8 x 180 ml/¾ cup ramekins

SERVES 8

First, dissolve the gelatin powder with a tablespoon of warm water.

Combine the cream, milk, sugar and vanilla seeds in a small saucepan over a medium heat, and bring to the boil. Reduce the heat and, stirring constantly, cook until the sugar has dissolved (about 5 minutes).

Remove from the heat and add the gelatin. Whisk until completely incorporated and set aside to cool.

Place the yogurt and lemon zest in a bowl and whisk together. Gradually pour in the cooled cream mixture, and continue to whisk until smooth. Pour the mixture into the ramekins and cover. Place in the refrigerator to set.

To serve, turn out each panna cotta onto a small serving plate. Top with a Fig Spoon Fruit and a drizzle of syrup.

Note You can also leave and serve the panna cotta in the bowls they set in – just top with figs and syrup.

FIG SPOON FRUIT

12 firm figs, rinsed
200 g/1 cup granulated/caster sugar
2 tablespoons port
still-warm sterilized glass jars with airtight lids

MAKES 475 ML/2 CUPS

In a non-reactive pan bring the sugar and 235 ml/ 1 cup of water to a boil over a medium-high heat. Reduce the heat and simmer for 10 minutes, stirring occasionally until the sugar has dissolved. Remove the pan from the heat and add the port. Stir, return the pan to the heat, and cook for a further 2 minutes. Add the figs, swirl the pan to coat and simmer for 10 minutes. Remove the pan from the heat and let the figs rest in the syrup for a further 10 minutes.

Spoon the figs and syrup into warm, sterilized, glass jars leaving a 5-mm/¼-inch space at the top. Seal the jars for 20 minutes following the method on page 4). Once sealed, store unopened in a cool, dark place for up to 12 months.

Lemon polenta cake

A deliciously tangy and lemony treat that just happens to be gluten-free.

200 g/1 stick plus
6 tablespoons butter
230 g/1 cup plus
2½ tablespoons golden
caster/raw cane sugar
3 eggs
200 g/1⅓ cups ground almonds
100 g/¾ cup polenta/cornmeal
1 teaspoon baking powder
3 lemons

LEMON ICING
1 tablespoon freshly squeezed
lemon juice
250 g/2 cups icing/
confectioners' sugar
*6 x 170-ml/6-oz. pudding
moulds, greased and
base-lined with a small
circle of baking parchment*

MAKES 8

Preheat the oven to 170°C (325°F) Gas 3.

Beat the butter and 200 g/1 cup of the sugar together in a large mixing bowl, until light and fluffy. Add the eggs, one at a time, beating well after each addition. Add small amounts of ground almonds if the mixture begins to curdle. Add in the remaining ground almonds and beat well.

Stir in the polenta/yellow cornmeal and baking powder. Add the grated zest and freshly squeezed juice of ½ a lemon and stir again.

Divide the batter evenly between the prepared pudding moulds and put them on a baking sheet. Bake in the preheated oven for 20 minutes or until a skewer inserted into a cake comes out clean.

Meanwhile, make a lemon syrup. Place the zest and juice of the remaining lemons in a saucepan set over a gentle heat, with the remaining sugar. Stir to combine and heat until the sugar has dissolved completely.

Remove the cakes from the oven and prick all over with a skewer. Pour the lemon syrup over each cake and let it soak through – about 1 tablespoon per cake.

Let cool in the pudding basins for 15 minutes before turning the cakes out to cool completely.

To make the lemon icing, add just enough lemon juice to the icing/confectioners' sugar for a thick but slightly runny consistency.

When ready to serve, spoon the lemon icing on top of cakes and let it drip down their sides.

Berry friands

These little cakes are particularly popular in Australia where you will find them on the counter in most coffee shops.

250 g/2 cups icing/
confectioners' sugar
50 g/6 tablespoons plain/
all-purpose flour
170 g/1¼ cups ground almonds
grated zest of 1 lemon
6 egg whites

200 g/1 stick plus 6 tablespoons
unsalted butter, melted
85 g/⅔ cup blueberries
85 g/⅔ cup raspberries
*a 12-hole non-stick friand or
muffin pan, well-greased*

MAKES 12

Preheat the oven to 180°C (350°F) Gas 4.

Sift the icing/confectioners' sugar and flour into a large mixing bowl, then stir through the ground almonds and lemon zest.

In a separate bowl, lightly beat the egg whites with a whisk or fork to break them up, then stir them through the dry ingredients to make a smooth paste.

Add half of the melted butter to the batter and stir well before adding the remaining butter.

Fold in half of the blueberries and raspberries, then divide the batter evenly in the pan – they should be two-thirds full. Place the remaining berries on top and bake in the preheated oven for 15–20 minutes, until firm and golden brown. Remove the pan from the oven and let it cool on a wire rack for about 10 minutes before turning the friands out. Serve.

Miso & sweet potato cheesecake

300 ml/2¼ cups double/heavy cream, whipped, to serve

ROASTED SWEET POTATO PURÉE

750 g/1⅔ lbs. raw sweet potato, skin on and cut into chunks

olive oil

BASE

120 g/4¼ oz. digestive biscuits/ graham crackers

140 g/5 oz. ginger biscuits/ cookies

1 tablespoon muscovado sugar

120 g/1 stick butter, plus extra for greasing

FILLING

500 g/2 cups plus 3 tablespoons cream cheese

60 g/4 tablespoons white miso paste

150 g/¾ cup caster/granulated sugar

1 vanilla pod/bean, seeds only

freshly squeezed juice of 1 lime

zest of 2 limes

1 quantity Roasted Sweet Potato Purée (see left)

5 eggs

2 extra egg yolks

23-cm/9-inch springform cake pan, lined with baking parchment and greased

SERVES 8–12

An unusual combination for a dessert but one that will surprise and delight. Don't worry if this cheesecake cracks – this is the case for most baked cheesecakes, expect imperfect perfection.

Preheat the oven to 200°C (400°F) Gas 6.

Start with the roasted sweet potato purée: toss the sweet potatoes with a drizzle of oil on a baking sheet and roast in the preheated oven for about 40 minutes.

Allow it to cool for a little while and peel of the skin. Place in a food processor and blitz until smooth.

Next, make the base: blitz the digestive biscuits/ graham crackers and ginger biscuits/cookies and the sugar to a medium-fine crumb in a food processor. Melt the butter and add to the biscuit/cookie crumbs. Pulse until just mixed. Tip the mixture into the cake pan, then press it evenly into the bottom of the pan. Bake for 10 minutes then leave to cool.

Turn the oven down to 180°C (350°F) Gas 4. Clean the bowl of the food processor. Add the cream cheese, miso paste, sugar, vanilla seeds, lime juice and zest and blend until smooth, scraping down the sides of the bowl. Add the Roasted Sweet Potato Purée, eggs and extra yolks and blend again until smooth, making sure you scrape down the sides of the bowl once more.

Pour this mixture into the cake pan and bake for 15 minutes. Reduce the temperature to 110°C (225°F) Gas ¼ and bake for a further 60–70 minutes. The cake is ready when it is set around the edges and slightly wobbly in the centre.

Remove from the oven and leave the cheesecake to cool in its pan on a wire rack for about 1 hour. Then, run a knife around the edges of the pan and carefully remove the ring. Slide the cheesecake onto a plate and leave to cool completely before serving.

Serve with whipped double/heavy cream.

Green tea madeleines WITH VANILLA & BLACK PEPPER CREAM

*Fluffy green shells with peppery cream clouds,
the former slightly warm and the latter nice
and chilled, makes for a dreamy combination.*

160 g/1 cup plus 2 tablespoons
    plain/all-purpose flour
1/4 teaspoon salt
1/2 teaspoon baking powder
1 tablespoon matcha green
    tea powder (the best quality
    you can find)
2 UK large, US extra large eggs
170 g/3/4 cup plus 2 tablespoons
    caster/granulated sugar
2 tablespoons freshly squeezed
    lime juice
125 g/1 stick plus 1 tablespoon
    butter, melted and cooled
zest of 2 limes
oil, for greasing

icing/confectioners' sugar,
    for dusting

**VANILLA & BLACK
PEPPER CREAM**
300 ml/1 1/4 cups double/
    heavy cream
1/2 vanilla pod/bean,
    seeds only
3–5 turns finely ground
    black pepper
splash of sake (optional)
icing/confectioners' sugar
    (if using sake)
2 x 9-hole madeleine pans

MAKES 18

In a medium bowl, sift together the flour, salt,
baking powder and matcha powder and set aside.

In a large bowl, whisk the eggs and sugar until
pale and doubled in volume, about 3–5 minutes.

Whisk the lime juice into the egg mixture then
fold in the flour mixture (using a spatula) until
just combined.

Fold in the melted butter and lime zest and
refrigerate for at least 1–2 hours.

Preheat the oven to 200°C (400°F) Gas 6, when
you are ready to cook the madeleines.

Grease the madeleine pans with a little oil and
spoon in the batter until the mixture comes about
three-quarters of the way up each mould.

Bake in the preheated oven for 12–15 minutes
until the madeleines are lightly golden around
the edges.

While the madeleines are cooking, make the
Vanilla & Black Pepper Cream by whisking the
cream into very soft peaks and folding in the vanilla
and black pepper. If using the sake add a very small
splash and sweeten to taste with a little icing/
confectioners' sugar.

Once the madeleines are done, transfer to a wire
rack to cool slightly. Serve the warm madeleines with
the cream.

Chocolate & salted caramel peanut slice

This treat brings back the wonder of childhood when you discovered that boiling a can of condensed milk created caramel. The salted peanuts help to cut through its intense sweetness and add a lovely crunch.

120 g/1 cup self-raising/rising flour
70 g/1 scant cup shredded/desiccated coconut
75 g/⅓ cup caster/ granulated sugar
110 g/7 tablespoons unsalted butter, melted

CARAMEL
1 x 395-g/14-oz. can sweetened condensed milk
120 g/1 stick unsalted butter
120 g/½ cup soft light brown sugar
100 g/⅔ cup roasted salted peanuts, roughly chopped

TOPPING
150 g/1¼ cups chopped dark/bittersweet chocolate
100 ml/scant ½ cup double/heavy cream
coarse sea salt, to decorate (optional)
a 20 x 30-cm/8 x 12-inch baking pan, greased and lined with baking parchment

SERVES 20–24

Preheat the oven to 180°C (350°F) Gas 4.

Place the flour, coconut and caster/granulated sugar in a large mixing bowl. Pour the melted butter over the dry ingredients, mix together and press firmly into the base of the prepared baking pan.

Bake in the preheated oven for about 15 minutes, or until light golden in colour. Remove from the oven and set aside to cool.

To make the caramel layer, place the unopened can of condensed milk on a folded kitchen towel in a deep saucepan or pot to stop it rattling while it boils. Cover completely with warm water, bring to the boil over a medium–high heat. Reduce the heat to low and simmer for 4 hours.

Remove from the water and allow the can to cool before opening it – the milk will have magically transformed into caramel.

In a separate saucepan or pot set over a medium heat, melt the butter with the light brown sugar, until the sugar has completely dissolved. Add the cooked condensed milk, reduce the heat and simmer for 10 minutes until the mixture has thickened slightly.

Pour the hot caramel mixture over the baked base and sprinkle the salted peanuts evenly across the top.

To make the topping, melt the chocolate and cream together in a heatproof bowl set over a pan of simmering water, making sure the base of the bowl doesn't touch the water below. Pour evenly over the caramel layer and chill in the fridge.

Once set, remove from the fridge and sprinkle with coarse sea salt. Cut into even square slices and serve stacked high on a plate.

Pavlova with strawberries & PASSION FRUIT CURD

Nothing says summer quite like pavlova. Crisp meringue with a marshmallowy centre, it's bright and bold, generous, unrefined, and always a crowd-pleaser.

6 egg whites

a pinch of salt

375 g/2 cups caster/superfine sugar

3 teaspoons cornflour/cornstarch

1½ teaspoons white wine vinegar

½ teaspoon pure vanilla extract

PASSION FRUIT CURD

4 passion fruit

1 large egg, plus 2 large egg yolks

115 g/½ cup plus 1 tablespoon
    caster/granulated sugar

75 g/5 tablespoons unsalted butter

1 teaspoon freshly squeezed lime juice

TOPPING

500 ml/2 cups whipping/heavy cream

5 passion fruit

300 g/3 cups fresh strawberries,
    hulled and halved

SERVES 6–8

To make the passion fruit curd, put the pulp of the passion fruit in a food processor and blitz to loosen the seeds. Strain into a jug/pitcher using a fine mesh sieve/strainer. Put the egg and egg yolks in a medium mixing bowl and whisk to combine. Set aside.

Put the butter with the sugar and strained passion fruit juice in a small heavy-bottomed saucepan or pot set over a gentle heat, and stir until the butter has melted and the sugar has dissolved. Pour one-third of the butter mixture into the whisked eggs, then return to the pan. Continue to cook gently, stirring continuously with a wooden spoon, until the mixture has thickened and coats the back of the spoon. It is important not to let the mixture get too hot as it will scramble the eggs and may curdle. Remove from the heat and stir through the lime juice and the pulp of the remaining passion fruit. Press a piece of clingfilm/plastic wrap onto the surface of the curd to prevent a skin forming and set in the fridge for 1 hour, or until chilled.

Preheat the oven to 180°C (350°F) Gas 4.

Draw a 25-cm/10-inch diameter circle onto a piece of baking parchment, then turn the paper over and place on a baking sheet.

In a clean, dry bowl, whisk the egg whites and salt to soft peaks. Add the sugar, one-third at a time, whisking after each addition until the peaks become stiff and shiny.

Sprinkle the cornflour/cornstarch, vinegar and vanilla over the whisked whites, and gently fold until just combined. Heap the meringue onto the baking parchment within the marked circle and use a large spoon to flatten the top and shape it into a round circle.

Place in the preheated oven and immediately reduce the heat to 150°C (300°F) Gas 2. Cook for 1¼ hours, then turn off the oven and leave the meringue to cool completely in the oven.

For the topping, whisk the cream until just whipped, then fold through half of the chilled passion fruit curd.

Turn the pavlova over onto a plate and peel off the baking parchment. Turn back over then spoon the passion fruit cream onto the meringue base. Layer with more passion fruit curd and top with fresh passion fruit pulp and strawberries.

ELDERBERRY CORDIAL

Elderflowers have beautiful frilly white blossoms. You wouldn't believe that such beauty can also make amazing drinks as well as producing a exotic cargo of berries which can be preserved.

450 g/2¼ cups white sugar
500 ml/2 cups boiling water
12 elderflower heads, rinsed

MAKES 700 ML/3 CUPS

Place the sugar in a large bowl and pour over the boiling water. Stir until the sugar is dissolved. Add the rinsed elderflower and stir to mix. Cover and set aside to cool overnight.

Strain the mixture through a cheesecloth/muslin or coffee filter into a pitcher/jug. Store in an airtight container in the refrigerator for up to 12 months.

Elderberry snow cones

These are grown-up snow cones laced with vodka. Almost too pretty to drink, the ice is crushed so finely it looks like snow. Dress them up with a pretty garnish of elderberries or blossom.

finely crushed ice
250 ml/1 cup vodka
Elderberry Cordial
  (see above), to top up

elderberries or blossoms,
  to garnish (optional)
4 glasses, chilled

SERVES 4

Fill the chilled glasses with crushed ice, then pour 60 ml/¼ cup of vodka into each glass. Top with Elderberry Cordial.

Garnish each glass with elderberries or blossom and serve.

Dark and stormy

This refreshing punch is hailed as the national drink of Bermuda. In this recipe a homemade ginger beer gives this drink a zestier flavour.

crushed ice
250 ml/1 cup Goslings Black
    Seal rum or similar
ginger beer (see below),
    to top up

lime wedges, to serve
chilli/chili flakes, to serve
    (optional)
4 glasses, chilled

SERVES 4

Fill the chilled glasses with crushed ice. Pour a 60 ml/¼ cup of rum into each glass and top with Ginger Beer. Finish each glass with a squeeze of lime and a pinch of chilli/chili flakes and enjoy!

OLD-FASHIONED GINGER BEER

2 x 11.5-cm/4½-inch pieces
    of fresh ginger, peeled and
    finely chopped
175 g/1¼ cups caster/superfine
    sugar
grated zest and juice of 1 lemon

1 teaspoon active dry yeast
*sterilized glass bottles with
    airtight caps or flip lids*

**MAKES 2 LITRES/
9 CUPS**

Bring 1.1 litres/5 cups of water, the ginger and sugar to a boil in a saucepan over a medium-high heat. Reduce the heat and simmer for 10 minutes, stirring occasionally until the sugar has dissolved. Remove from the heat and cool until the liquid is just warm.

Add the lemon zest, juice and the yeast. Stir and cover with a lid. Set aside in a warm place for 24 hours.

Strain the ginger beer through a cheesecloth/ muslin or coffee filter into sterilized bottles. Loosely screw the caps on and set aside in a cool, dark place for 3 days before serving. Store in the refrigerator for up to 4 days.

Lime, cucumber and lychee gin and tonic

The combination of lime, cucumber and lychee is just magical – light, fresh, floral and with a gentle sweetness. A perfect pre-dinner drink.

200 ml/scant 1 cup lychee juice
200 ml/scant 1 cup gin
½ cucumber, cut into thick slices
1 can lychees in syrup, drained
3 sprigs of mint, leaves picked

2 limes, sliced
ice cubes
cocktail sticks/toothpicks

SERVES 6

Mix the lychee juice and gin in a jug/pitcher and add some ice. Take the cocktail sticks/toothpicks and thread on a piece of cucumber and a lychee and set aside.

Place some ice into the glasses, pour over the gin mixture, garnish with lime slices and mint leaves and top with a lychee and cucumber cocktail stick/toothpick.

Best ever bloody mary

This is the ultimate brunch drink, allowing you to ingest booze before midday with complete legitimacy and even a hint of sophistication.

500 ml/2 cups tomato juice
30 ml/2 tablespoons
   Worcestershire sauce
30 ml/2 tablespoons
   Sriracha chilli sauce
a 3-cm/1¼-inch piece of
   horseradish, finely grated
sea salt and freshly ground
   black pepper

60 ml/¼ cup freshly squeezed
   lime juice
300 ml/1¼ cups vodka

TO GARNISH
Pickled Celery (see right)
chilli/chile flakes

SERVES 4

Put the tomato juice into a jug/pitcher and stir in the Worcestershire sauce, Sriracha chilli sauce and grated horseradish. Season with salt and pepper, cover with clingfilm/plastic wrap and chill in the fridge for at least 30 minutes.

When ready to serve, add the lime juice and vodka, and stir well. Place a pickled celery stick in 6 high-ball glasses, fill each glass with ice and pour in the Bloody Mary mixture. Garnish each with a pinch of chilli/chile flakes and enjoy!

Green tea granita

Kick back in the summer heat with a glass of this refreshing green tea magic. Take it to your sun lounger with a straw and a spoon. If you want to take this healthful granita to another level, free-pour some chilled sake over the top – Kanpai!

4 good-quality green tea bags,
   or 2 tablespoons loose-leaf
   green tea
1 handful fresh mint, finely
   chopped
2.5-cm/1-inch piece of fresh
   ginger, peeled and sliced

small pinch of cayenne pepper
freshly squeezed juice of
   1 lemon
runny honey, to taste
fresh mint leaves, to serve

SERVES 4–6

Put 750 ml/3 cups water in a saucepan over a high heat. Once almost boiling, add the tea, mint, ginger and cayenne pepper then cover and turn off the heat. Leave to sit for 10 minutes to infuse then strain through a fine sieve/strainer to remove the solids.

Add the lemon juice and honey to taste.

Pour the liquid into a plastic or glass container and place in the freezer for at least 3–4 hours. It is important that every 30 minutes you stir the mixture with a fork to break up the ice crystals.

When ready to serve, if you find the mixture is too slushy, give it a good stir and return to the freezer until more solid, or if you find it is too hard just remove it from the freezer for a few minutes until softened slightly.

Serve in glasses garnished with fresh mint leaves.

PICKLED CELERY

1 head celery, peeled and
 trimmed to sticks taller
 than your serving glass
500 g/2½ cups caster/
 granulated sugar
1 litre/4 cups white wine vinegar
2 tablespoons sea salt
8 garlic cloves, chopped

2 teaspoons mustard seeds
2 teaspoons chilli/hot red
 pepper flakes
2 teaspoons black peppercorns
*sterilized, glass jars with
 airtight lids*

MAKES 500 ML/2 CUPS

Stand the celery sticks in a tall, sterilized, glass jar.
Place the remaining ingredients in a saucepan or
pot with 250 ml/1 cup of water. Set over a medium–
high heat and bring to the boil. Continue to boil for
15 minutes, remove from the heat and cover to stop
the liquor evaporating. Set aside to cool slightly,
then pour into the jar with the celery sticks. Wipe
the jar clean and tightly screw on the lid. Turn upside
down and leave until completely cold.
The celery is best made a day or two
in advance.

Index

Picture credits

Peter Cassidy Pages 40, 48, 55, 143, 149

Richard Jung Page 65

Mowie Kay Pages 11, 15, 28, 52, 79, 80, 84, 86, 91, 126

Erin Kunkel Pages 3, 36, 58, 59, 67, 75, 99, 100, 102, 103, 104, 107, 111, 112, 114, 116, 117, 139, 152, 155, 156, 157, 168, 169, 170, 171

Steve Painter Pages 17, 18, 129

Con Poulos Pages 38, 53, 120, 125, 133, 134, 137, 142, 162, 163

William Reavell Page 14

Yuki Sugiura Pages 34, 35, 76, 122, 141, 145

Debi Treloar Pages 5, 110, 158

Ian Wallace Pages 68, 71, 83, 94, 95, 108

Kate Whitaker Pages 1, 12, 13, 20, 24, 27, 31, 43, 44, 45, 50, 51, 60, 63, 64, 92, 146, 147, 150, 151, 166, 173

Isobel Wield Pages 2, 88

Claire Winfield Page 41

Getty Images Pages 3, 7, 8–9, 10, 19, 22, 23, 29, 30, 37, 46, 56–57, 61, 73, 86–97, 101, 110, 111, 118–119, 121, 130, 131, 138, 158, 159

Alamy Pages 32–33, 39, 47, 69, 72, 87, 115, 146–147

Recipe credits

Valerie Aikman-Smith
Charmoula paste
Coconut & lime shrimp skewers
Cucumber pickles
Dark & stormy
Elderberry cordial
Elderberry snow cones
Garden herb butter
Grilled halloumi with jalapeno, lime & tequila relish
Grilled harissa chicken kabobs
Korean steak & noodles
Grilled lobsters with flavoured butters
Garlic chilli shrimp
Grilled market vegetable salad with herbed toasts
Matcha ice cream with black sesame praline
Mexican grilled corn
Ouzo watermelon salad
Pickled kaffir limes
Spanish sherry marinade
Spiced red snapper with charmoula
Spicy dark chocolate & coconut pots
Spicy grilled salmon collar
Spicy peanut noodles
Sriracha & lime grilled chicken wings
Summer chicken with nectarine agrodolce
Tutti frutti semifreddo with candied citrus
West coast crab cakes
Yogurt panna cotta with fig spoon fruit

Vatcharin Bhumichitr
Coconut ice cream
Lychee sorbet
Papaya salad with squid
Thai fruit salad
Vegetables with spicy dip of young chillies
Vermicelli salad

Jordan Bourke
Charred shrimp with nam jim
Coconut frozen yogurt with strawberries
Crab with mango & coconut
Grated carrots, blood orange & walnuts

Mojito sorbet
Tempura vegetables & shrimp with wasabi mayonnaise

Felipe Fuentes Cruz & Ben Fordham
Beer-battered avocado dippers
Guacamole

Tori Haschka
Fish tacos with chipotle-lime crema

Atsuko Ikeda
Chicken teriyaki with lime on quinoa rice
Fried & steamed salmon in miso garlic sauce
Miso-glazed aubergine
Simmered beef & tomatoes on rice
Tofu steaks with sesame & soy dressing

Kathy Kordalis
Blackberry & blueberry açai bowl
Glow balls
Grainy porridge
Lime, cucumber & lychee gin & tonic
Sourdough toast toppings: crushed berries & goat's curd; avocado & salmon; broad bean, courgette & goat's curd
Spinach & ricotta dip with flatbreads
Whipped honey vanilla butter

Louise Pickford
Beef Bulgogi & rice noodle wraps
Ember-roasted potatoes
Kaffir lime, squid & noodle salad
Mee grob
Prawn & beef satays
Ssamjang sauce
Steamed rice noodle dumplings with scallops
Szechuan chilli dressing

James Porter
'Ahi katsu
Basic sushi rice
Kalua chipotle ketchup
Lobster quesadillas
Pickled ginger
Pipikaula
Sticky aubergine poke with sour carrot salad
Teriyaki burger

Yuzu lomi lomi salmon poke
Yuzu-mango salsa

Shelagh Ryan
Asian chicken noodle salad
Banana bread with raspberry labne
Berry friands
Best-ever bloody Mary
Chocolate & salted caramel peanut slice
Corn fritters with roast tomatoes & smashed avocados
Courgette loaf
French toast with honey roast figs, orange mascarpone & toasted almonds
Grilled squid salad with herb lime dressing
Lemon polenta cake
Pavlova with strawberries & passion fruit curd
Pickled celery
Shaved fennel salad with walnuts, Parmesan & pomegranate
Spicy pork burger with mango salsa
Toasted muesli with baked rhubarb

Laura Santini
Garlic, chilli & parsley prawns
Glass noodle, shiitake & vegetable steam-fry
Green tea granita
Green tea madeleines with vanilla & black pepper cream
Grilled lamb koftas
Maple & bacon pancakes
Miso & sweet potato cheesecake
Monkfish with mango & avocado salsa
Quinoa & asparagus salad with matcha lemon dressing
Sake mussels
Savoury granola
Spicy tuna & black rice bowl
Sunshine laksa with crab & snow peas
Sweet potato, smoked mackerel & grapefruit salad
Thai-steamed snapper with sticky coconut jasmine rice

Janet Sawyer
Apple & blueberry waffles
Hand-dived scallops with vanilla risotto & pea shoots
Sweet potato pancakes with cinnamon & vanilla